Diane Ackerman

Reverse Thunder

A Dramatic Poem

Reverse Thunder

Diane Ackerman

REVERSE THUNDER

Lumen Books

Excerpts from this work have appeared in *The American Poetry Review* and *The Denver Quarterly.*

Lumen Books
446 West 20 Street
New York, NY 10011

© 1988 Lumen, Inc.

Printed in the United States of America
ISBN 0-930829-09-3

Lumen Books are produced by Lumen, Inc., a tax-exempt, non-profit organization providing design and editorial services to other non-profit agencies. This publication is made possible in part, with public funds from the New York State Council on the Arts, the National Endowment for the Arts, and with private contributions.

Reverse Thunder

Preface

Sister Juana Inés de la Cruz was an extraordinary woman who had the bad fortune to live during an era which demanded that its women be ordinary. She was a child prodigy with a gift and passion for learning at a time when education was not available for women. She was a natural scientist who conducted experiments in her convent cell at a time when the Catholic Church felt deeply threatened by the discoveries of Galileo, Newton, Harvey, and others. She disagreed with some points of theological doctrine at a time when women were forbidden to take part in Church philosophy. She taught the younger nuns such subjects as theology, physics, mathematics, logic, astronomy, music, philosophy, and art at a time when formal study by women, let alone nuns, was thought to undermine the social structure and contradict the laws of God.

As if all that were not enough, she also wrote daring poetry and plays, in one of which she compares the ancient Indian ritual of the sacrifice of the Corn God to the death and resurrection of Christ and the Sacrament of Communion. Such a modern idea, which made the double offense of taking seriously the Indians' pagan religion and dabbling in comparative theology, infuriated the seventeenth-century Catholic Church, and was used against her in her ultimate downfall. Even if she were not one of the most famous Spanish poets of the seventeenth century, whose plays, poetry, and prose have influenced writers and fascinated readers ever since, her turbulent life, full of confrontation, intellectual poise, and a tragic fight for the right of all women to be educated, would secure her place in history.

Juana Inés de Asbaje was born in the Mexican countryside in 1648(?), to a Creole mother and a Spanish father who never formally married. Her father deserted her mother when Juana was a baby, and so her childhood was spent in her grandfather's house, where a well-stocked library became her preoccupation. By three, she had learned to read and write; by seven, she had taught herself Latin and was reading the ancients. From then on, her learning snowballed until, finally, she begged her mother to let her cut her hair, dress as a boy, and attend the (all-male) university at Mexico City. To her family that was unthinkable. Learning was considered indelicate and, at the very least, useless for a girl, since, in truth, she had only two futures open to her: marriage or the convent. Juana went to Mexico City anyway, but as a lady-in-waiting at court, where her world would be wider and she might make contacts useful for an advantageous marriage. Contemporary writers spoke of her wit, modesty, and beauty, which may be why she rose so quickly in the affections of all at court, because soon she became lady-in-waiting to the Viceroy's wife, and poet laureate—two unusual honors for a Creole. Though little is known about her life at this time, there is a record of the Viceroy's inviting forty professors from the university to test her learning publicly, and a report that she bested them "like a galleon being attacked by canoes." Her beauty and wit soon were famous, she undoubtedly had many suitors, and her poetry suggests romantic intrigues. Unfortunately, ladies-in-waiting grow to marriage age, and Juana found herself in a dilemma. She could give up her personal and intellectual freedom and marry, or she could become a nun. So repugnant was the thought of being virtually owned by a husband who would almost certainly curtail her studies that, at sixteen, she entered a convent. Apparently, convent life was also difficult, because she left it a little later without taking her vows. Within a year, she had entered another, more liberal convent, St. Jerome, where she stayed the rest of her life.

It was in St. Jerome that the real drama and tragedy of her life began. Some of the Mexican orders of nuns were remarkably modern, and much less strict than their European counterparts. In St. Jerome, the nuns received visitors and entertained, had swarms of servants who carried messages to and from the court (and courtiers), held fiestas on religious holidays, wrote and staged plays, and generally became the center of the province's thriving social life. The more worldly the convent became, the more the Church bristled. The seventeenth century was a time of intellecutal commotion. Thanks to the "New Science," people's concept of nature and religious teachings was changing swiftly. The Church insisted that the earth was the center of the universe, and Galileo said it was one world among many. The Church insisted that fossils were put into rocks by God to test our faith in Genesis, and biologists like John Ray said they were the remains of dead organisms. Scientific societies were springing up all over Europe, and the first scientific journals being published. The telescope, microscope, and other instruments of study were invented and improved, and people round the world were using them. If the earth was no longer the center of the universe, the Church was no longer the sole interpreter of nature. It was a period of intellectual excitement, when every year seemed replete with new discoveries, and the Church felt desperately uneasy. Sister Juana Inés de la Cruz was right in the middle of the struggle. In her convent cell, she amassed the largest library in the New World, conducted experiments (some of which overlapped with Newton's), taught profane subjects such as astronomy and philosophy, was a musician and a painter, wrote love poetry, and lived the life of a Renaissance thinker. She became so well known and respected that European scientists and savants kept in constant touch with her through letters and messengers; they supplied her library, and sent her the latest scientific instruments. Ambassadors to the Viceroy's court frequently stopped at St. Jerome *first* to offer greetings from one friend and admirer or another. Apparently, she was also well-loved by the people of Mexico City, who found in her a modest, self-sacrificing woman who understood the needs of the poor because she had come from them. Thus she was able to live a rich life, keep up with all the whirlwind science of her day, read books in half a dozen languages, and, as is clear from her theological writings, be a devout and sensitive Christian. Some of her love poetry, which scholars have traditionally read as being about the body of Christ, is unusually sensual, and suggests that her amorous life continued while she was in the convent, which was not at all uncommon for nuns of her day. It must have seemed to her the best of all possible worlds.

The tide had been going against her for some time before she knew it. Deeply threatened by the new science, the Catholic Church found a woman practitioner of it an outrage. That she had dared to have opinions on Church doctrine was unforgivable. After Vespers one evening, in the course of discussion and refreshments, which habitually followed it at St. Jerome, a clergyman asked her opinion on a fashionable sermon by a Portuguese Jesuit. She disagreed with the sermon, and said so, deferentially, but in detail. The clergyman pressed her to jot down her argument so that he might study it at his leisure, assuring her that it would be kept for his eyes alone. As he was her superior, she agreed, adding that, though she disagreed with the sermon, others were more than welcome to disagree with her. Now we find her openness modern and fair-minded: each to his own opinion; but at the time disagreeing with a venerable Church Father, even for another Church Father, was daring, and for a nun it was close to blasphemy. The argument she jotted down suddenly appeared as a book, which made its way to the Bishop of Puebla, a man surrounded by panicky extremists. The Bishop applauded her intelligence, but not her worldly use of it, and gave her a severe reprimand along with strict orders that all visitors to the convent be sent away, and her time turned from study to prayer and penitence. All at once her life and motives were called into question, and in a letter now famous in the Spanish-speaking world, thanks to which we know the little we do about her early life, she told the Bishop about her childhood and innermost feelings, how she came to have the "black beast" of her curiosity, which she'd tried vainly to rid herself of lifelong.

It is an extraordinary document, at once learned and demure, but also painfully candid, as she tries to understand how so devilish a drive could have developed in her when all the world was against it. Modestly, deferentially, she nonetheless refused to give up her studies. Perhaps the Church feared that she would inspire other maidens to such unfit practices; perhaps she merely focussed its nervousness about the scientific revolution. Whatever the motives, the Bishop and his men did something to her in 1694. We do not know what exactly, nor if it was solely their efforts that broke her spirit. Her poems, so full of life and passion, stop at that point. Suddenly her will snapped and she gave way; all of her books and experiments were sold, and she was allowed to keep only a Bible and penitential hair shirts. The last four years of her life she spent in that solitary, bereft state, assiduously nursing the other nuns, most of whom were dying of the plague, until, as if she wished it so, she herself died of it in 1699. A number of her writings, miraculously, have survived. In *Reverse Thunder*, I have tried to imagine the most turbulent part of her life: some of it I have based on the writings themselves, and on what little we know about her; but other parts I have simply created from what I have come to understand of the woman's passions and where they might have led her. Her relationship with Giorgio is wholly invented. The play takes place during her convent years when, as an adult, she came to power and fell in love, then had to confront the many forces that would bring her down.

Diane Ackerman
Ithaca, N.Y.
September 1987

REVERSE THUNDER

Setting: Mexico, 1690. Sister Juana's convent cell, filled with experiments, scientific instruments appropriate to the seventeenth century, exotic objects from foreign lands, musical instruments, samples of wildlife, an in-progress painting on a stand. Overstuffed bookcases line the walls. Most of the props are at the rear of the stage, so that they can be hidden by a backdrop when the scene changes. At the front of the stage are a writing desk, a narrow bed, chairs, and a heap of books. Backdrops change the scene to Giorgio's chamber at court in Act II, the beach at Veracruz in Act I, Scene 2, and a more spartan convent cell in Act III, Scene 1.

Dramatis Personae

Sister Juana Inés de la Cruz, a sister in the Convent of St. Jerome near Mexico City. A creole beauty.

María, a young nun and servant to Juana

Giorgio, an Italian ambassador to the Viceroy's court

Viceroy, highest political leader in Mexico, appointed by the king of Spain

Mother Superior, prioress of the Convent of St. Jerome

Father Marceno, local clergyman

Ricardo, servant to Giorgio

Father Suárez, one of the bishop's men

Bishop of Puebla

Archbishop, highest religious leader in Mexico

Cabrera, a Mexican portrait painter

Nuns, courtiers, servants, and gentlemen

ACT I, Scene 1

Sister Juana's cell. JUANA and the MOTHER SUPERIOR are center stage. Miscellaneous NUNS wait nearby.

MOTHER SUPERIOR
Heaven knows, I've been lenient, Sister Juana,
because of your good heart and extraordinary gifts.

JUANA
(Too quickly)
No one could be less deserving, or more grateful.

MOTHER SUPERIOR
When you wanted to dissect those putrid water-hens.

JUANA
Egrets.

MOTHER SUPERIOR
Those egrets, whose necks were so swollen, red,
and wobbling with disease, I could barely
keep my breakfast porridge down to think of them
on the table there, oozing and rancid,
did I stop you?

JUANA
No, you were especially good about the egrets.

MOTHER SUPERIOR
When you sawed off the edge of every beam
in the vestibule . . .

JUANA
We were studying perspective, and . . .

MOTHER SUPERIOR
So that poor Father Vadra stood under
a trickle of plaster all during mass,
like Samson waiting to have his brains dashed out.

JUANA
(Offers her some water)
You were wonderful about the beams.
Here, you'll feel better if you drink this.

MOTHER SUPERIOR
(Drinks a little)

I've sewn wide pockets around you
in the cloth of my sacred duty,
Sister Juana, but there will be
no Greek play about incest and murder!

JUANA
(Curtseys)
Yes, Holy Mother.

MOTHER SUPERIOR
My heart won't take it, and, what's more to the point,
neither will the Bishop's.

JUANA
The Bishop of Puebla
has a fine, Christian sense of drama.

MOTHER SUPERIOR
It's the acts of those who surround him
that bother me. Some of them are like lightning bolts
scouting the province for a place to land.
I'd just as soon it not be here.

JUANA
(Helping her offstage)
Oh, no worry of that, and no Greek tragedy,
I promise.
(Returning)
Well . . .

SECOND NUN
(Disappointed)
No blood-curdling scream?

JUANA
It was a grand scream, Sister Marguerita.
We'll find another play
with a juicy scream in it for you,
but something a little tamer and more devout.
A saint's life perhaps.
(Consults her library. Bells ring.)

FIRST NUN
Oh, time already. Couldn't we miss devotions
today, and stay with you a little longer?

SECOND NUN
Please, Sister, please.

JUANA
No, no, butterflies, off with you, hurry.
God will give you better lines to speak.

THIRD NUN
Mathematics later?

JUANA
Yes, lessons later . . . *if* your duties are finished.

*(Three NUNS leave. JUANA and her servant, MARÍA, remain.
JUANA looks for a suitable play, as MARÍA picks up the fallen
helmets and swords. Squatting, MARÍA pushes a sword across the
stage, watching it, thinking. JUANA turns in time to see her
launch the second one.)*

JUANA
If looks had sound, your face would be mumbling.
What's the puzzle?

MARÍA
How far it would travel, if I pushed
even harder, as hard as a dozen armies, say.

JUNA
How far would you like it to go?

MARÍA
Across the ocean, across the world, forever even.

JUANA
Ah, forever, that makes it difficult.

MARÍA
I thought as much.

JUANA
Difficult, but not impossible,
according to Mr. Galileo.

MARÍA
The Greeks say that, in time, all things
stop moving but the stars.

JUANA

I know they do. And common sense agrees.
It's a lesson even a child dragging a toy
swiftly learns: things must be pushed.

MARÍA

Except animals, perhaps, or the wind?

JUANA

No, animals have whims and hungers, too,
so are human in that way. And the wind
that, like a violent husband, we know
even in its absence by the marks it leaves,
spurs motion, isn't bridled itself.
You've seen blown leaves, matting in wagonwheels
and ditches, how when they rush against
a wall, they stop like severed hands.
That rock I saw you fling at Mother's dog
yesterday . . .

MARÍA

Oh!

JUANA

. . . when you thought me at chapel,
fell to earth like a dead bird, stayed there.
Only the stars appear to glide forever
over the fat black of the sky, like boats
between launch and harbor, or no launch
and no harbor. So the Greeks have found that world
perfect, this one flawed. No surprise in that.
What we begin we can only imagine
ending, for such is our weakness
that when we set a thing in motion,
be it stone or child, soon enough it will stop.
    (Pauses)
No, the odd thought, the one against the senses,
was Galileo's: that the world works
as the heavens do, like two masons with one order.
And what cheek! That he should dare to prove it
not with everyday stuffs of this world,
the very world his new rules would redraw,
for bed or cabinets or washbasins of tin,

pushed across the room, will stop when pushing does.
No, his proof is balls on polished surfaces.
And, incidentally, he adds, we must ignore
that in the end these balls stop, too,
and, incidentally, must ignore that they tumble
end over end, not glide. You wonder
the Church Fathers growled! It beggars belief.

MARÍA
And yet you *do* believe about this
"inertia"; and also about the Earth's moving . . .
  (Looks about worrisomely)

JUANA
I don't find it unthinkable that God,
who lathed the world, might have left
the ball spinning.

  (A courtier, GIORGIO, who has been listening just out of sight, enters, startling them.)

GIORGIO
Take care, Sister. Where I come from,
heresy has ears.

JUANA
And where on earth *do* you come from?
Your clothes say it's likelier one of Galileo's worlds.

GIORGIO
If you mean I look heavenly, I'm much obliged.
In truth, I come from Turin, below the Alps;
which is nearly as high as Galileo's worlds, I admit,
but a few days closer. Not many.

JUANA
Come sit, then, and tell me all that's new
in Turin, not "who" but "what," unless the who
made the what, or the what was thought by a who.

GIORGIO
I don't think my satchel had room
for all those owls. Would you settle
for what brings me to you, for openers?

JUANA
For openers.

GIORGIO

I've come as an ambassador
to the Viceroy's court, but call on you first
at the request of Dr. Malpighi, your ardent admirer,
who tells me that through your cells here
pass all the wonders of the world, the news,
the sciences, the arts; that your library boasts
four thousand books . . . and glancing around, I see
that he was short of fingers for his sum.

JUANA

It kept his abacus spinning.

GIORGIO

In your study, I feel small as History
that here and there picks out a title or two,
construes the gloom for a moment,
an author, a cobweb, and leaves the rest a mystery.
Perhaps later you'd permit me to graze
a while over such well-grained steppes.

JUANA

Is your mind a nomad then?

GIORGIO

Each day, I find it pitching its small tent
elsewhere, moving from one field to the next.
But now we return to the subject I overheard.
You were speaking of motion, and I noted
that where I come from heresy has ears.

JUANA

(Shrugs)
It's heresy to be in on a day like this.

GIORGIO

So it is . . . I noticed you have blackbirds
hanging around your garden, weighing down
the apple trees like big, feathered fruits.
Quite startled me at first, to enter
a convent yard, and find a morality play on a tree.

JUANA

Indeed!
(She rushes to the window.)

You're right.
Such a vision. And that one branch swinging low
like a censer. I won't have it! María,
go chase the birds away, or ask them
"to pitch their tents elsewhere."
(MARÍA leaves)
What a day: to breathe is to draw in silk
through your nose as those orientals do.

GIORGIO
(Glancing at the books)
Sounds like Marco Polo
is one of your pages.

JUANA
All the pages in two editions,
the son very unlike the father, though.
(She pulls a book from the shelf.)
Here's a modish text you might like:
Luis de Góngora y Argote. Do you know him?

GIORGIO
Not yet. What's he like?

JUANA
(Considers)
A little like waking up inside
a hair shirt . . .

GIORGIO
Uh, huh.

JUANA
. . . that turns out to be a cow's cud
rotting in a meadow. I adore him.

GIORGIO
Partial to rotting cuds, are you?

JUANA
Odd things are manna to a soul in the wilderness.

GIORGIO
Your cow's begun to turn the clods
of my stomach, not the dirt.

8

JUANA
"If Ye had not plowed with my heifer,
ye had not found out my riddle."

GIORGIO
Ecclesiastes?

JUANA
Judges. But you've not told me your news.

GIORGIO
Nor will at this pace. I'd much sooner
sit knitting niceties with you,
but I'm afraid I must be off to tattle at court.

JUANA
Borrow this book, if you like.
"Go not empty unto thy mother-in-law."

GIORGIO
Please, no more Judges.

JUANA
Then, pardon me, sir.
Does that apply also to ecclesiastics?

GIORGIO
If you don't take offense by it,
I find you more like a sister than a nun.
Indeed, the nuns here have more servants
than court ladies do, if fewer dresses.

JUANA
Nor are they short on suits.

GIORGIO
That I would believe. As I entered,
I overheard two speaking of some trip you plan.

JUANA
To the coast, to explore the shallows,
where coral castles rise between the tides,
and fabulous things are: purple sponges
that ink the water when you squeeze them,
carp the size of shoes, crystal bladders
that do sting if you touch them,

but otherwise float like fairy pillows
from one rainbow to the next . . .

GIORGIO
Incredible! You've been there before.

JUANA
Oh, often as a child. The sea was my nursery,
and its green waves breaking like glass, trinkets.
At night, water cymbals were my lullaby.
And, but for the mosquitoes that hugged the beach
solely for the gift of our blood, it would seem,
I spent my happiest hours there,
prying into the lives of shelled things,
making seaweed crowns, paddling to the reef.

GIORGIO
How is it you never drowned?

JUANA
First, I dressed in men's clothes,
when I had a mind to go wading
and scrambling about. And second,
I learned from sailors in our town
how to lie on top of the water and swim.

GIORGIO
Rare thing, a sailor who wishes
a woman to lie
     (She scolds him with a look.)
. . . on the water and swim.
This is quickly becoming quite a salty tale.
I mean it wags wetly.

JUANA
My *brother* was a sailor, and shipbuilder, too.
Often he took me on his boat with him,
and when the coast winds bosomed in our sails
hardly a man on shore didn't spy us,
my brother with me beside, and dream
of setting sail.

GIORGIO
Unlikely past for a sister, or a nun.

JUANA

Well, if my younger days were unnunnish,
it better suits me. To know this world well,
there's Heaven in all its marvels;
and far above, the stars, padding into night
like pale cats down an alleyway,
beyond which, faith teaches us, lies
a greater Heaven still. If it be greater,
it must be greater than that Heaven
which greets me here, so, in proportion,
the sweeter I find earth's pomegranates
the more do I reaffirm the joys of Heaven,
since Heaven, by definition, exceeds all
earthly charms. A worldly woman
knows Heaven as the suburb of each day,
just as a courtier, such as you,
having tried on the satin splendors of court,
in their absence, I wager, will make do
with the poor pleasures of Genoa.

GIORGIO

(Laughs)

And lately I come from both
that world and that suburb. The scramble
over fish and coral you described,
were you able to leave today, I'd be
honored, delighted, to accompany you,
and from there bustle off to court.
And if, as you say, it would be heresy
to be indoors on a day like this,
I'd hate to be the cause of your ruin.

JUANA

A grand idea. I'll go fetch my things.
(JUANA leaves.)

GIORGIO

And I thought sailing to this world
I'd have monsters to reckon with.
There's a dragon rolling in my wrist
right now . . . God help me, I've heard
of chickens born without bones,
rocks that spit fire, camels passing

11

through a needle's eye, and other paradoxes
too weird, wicked, or fabulous to tell,
but nothing I would have credited less
than finding such an angel in a nun's cell.

CURTAIN

ACT I, Scene 2

On the beach at Veracruz, JUANA and GIORGIO are sitting on the rocks, tossing pebbles into the water. She is wearing a tunic that he has lent her. Her face is a bit sunburned, her hair short. A shimmery spotlight gives the sense of the sun. Sound of waves and gulls. GIORGIO picks up a rock and skips it across the water: pinpoint stage-lights give the effect of a skipping stone. JUANA laughs, impressed.

GIORGIO
Oh, I can do better than that.
    (Stands up, finds a stone of just the right shape, and steps deeply to pitch it)

JUANA
    (Applauds)
Wonderful! Seven skips.
Why do you suppose it does that?

GIORGIO
What?

JUANA
Skate along, not penetrate the water.

GIORGIO
Madam, such talk around young men!
Although, at the moment, you do look a bit
lad-like yourself.
    (Juana feigns affront.)
Well, with the shirt and the short hair.

JUANA
You don't like my hair short.

GIORGIO
I'd like you bald as a melon.

JUANA
I nearly was once, when I was so high.
To teach me to learn my lessons better.

GIORGIO
When you were so high? Not *so* high?
    (Gestures higher)

JUANA

No, no, like a wild animal, I clambered
to my feet soon after I was born.
By three, I'd learned to read and when, at six,
or seven, I forget which, I overheard
a guest mention the university
I begged my mother to let me go there,
hair cropped short and dressed like a boy,
since only boys could go.

GIORGIO

And so you cut your hair. I'm surprised to hear
your mother allowed it.

JUANA

She didn't. God's faith, I wailed and kicked,
I ate only cheese for a week, I filled
my mouth with chalk and frothed as if mad,
then I locked myself up and wouldn't eat
for days but in the end her stronger will
and common sense prevailed.

GIORGIO

As it should with a raw girl.

JUANA

I suppose. But it meant I had to be
my own tutor, as well as pupil and best friend,
and what a lonely cavalcade of selves
that was. In my grandfather's library,
which, to everyone's dismay, was my favorite toy,
I began to study Latin from the texts
in whose margins he'd scribbled,
and found such a banquet for my senses there
that a madness to somehow know it all
overwhelmed me.

GIORGIO

You're not the first to give in to such gluttony.

JUANA

The first woman in this prim world, for all
the fuss it made, makes still in some quarters.

GIORGIO
Your hair?

JUANA
My madness grew so strong, and so perverse,
that, even though a woman's hair is dear
to her, especially in the solstice of youth
when the sun is always at high noon,
and the tarantulas of vanity
are on the prowl, I measured my hair,
cut off two or three inches, and swore
if it grew back that far without my knowing
this lesson or that in some thorny text,
I'd slice it off again as punishment.
As it turned out, the hair grew back
long before I learned what I proposed,
since hair grows fast, and I learned slowly.
So, off it came! It just didn't seem right
to dress a head so naked of knowledge
in such finery.

GIORGIO
How strict for a child: to be her own tormentor.
Why were you so stern?

JUANA
Not with others, only myself.
I've often wondered why. It scares me now.

GIORGIO
Forgive such an impertinence, for in truth
I've known you less than a week,
if well in that time. But you seem . . .
an unlikely woman to be a nun.

JUANA
Would I be more likely as a wife,
with Descartes and Aristotle in my husband's bed?

GIORGIO
No.

JUANA
Well, there you have it.

GIORGIO
You lived at court once.

JUANA
Yes, for a short time, a lady-in-waiting
to the Viceroy's wife.

GIORGIO
Quite a famous time from what I'm told,
eloping with the hearts of all the young courtiers,
writing plays, fencing wits.

JUANA
Oh, that sweet gossip's a confection for the most part.
It's true, I had suitors enough, but they
all seemed so unsubtle, so incurious, so solemn.
They knew all the mired roads
between their bedposts and their taverns,
but not one could say where his liver was.
Their worlds were small as nooses.
How could I marry and be chained to a cradle,
when all the universe was out there
gibbering and fidgeting and wailing to be seen?

GIORGIO
A ripe rose doesn't wait long in a court garden.

JUANA
No. And the pressure was dreadful.

GIORGIO
Your father?

JUANA
He left us, ran off, when I was just born.
Mother never speaks of him. But she and grandfather,
in whose house we lived, they were keen.
The Viceroy was keen. The suitors were keen.
My father confessor was keen. *I* alone was blunt.
I remember that time very well: it was winter,
and there were evergreens in the courtyard
on whose spires the sky looked impaled.
Each limb spread feathery hands and rocked in the wind,
as if motioning me to be seated.
And my heart kept circling like the dog it was,

16

unable to find a fit place to settle.
I'm afraid it was a miserable season to bloom in.

GIORGIO
But to become a nun, the other extreme.

JUANA
No, no, our convents are not so strict
as you imagine. Certain orders here
are as close to court as you are, closer
to some courtiers. As you saw, we have servants
of all colors and callings, who wait on us,
and travel between the convent and the court
as stealthily as colds. We entertain,
we house pilgrims, we compose plays
for fiestas and religious holidays.
After Vespers, Friday evenings, we do
as the ancient Hebrews did, and meet friends
for supper, gossip, and theological discussion.

GIORGIO
Our nuns in Europe tie their laces tighter.

JUANA
So I hear. Truly, we lead austere lives
given mainly to prayer, devotion, and good works,
but we're no order of prim, tight-mouthed viragos.
The radius of our world, thank God, is much wider,
even if we don't all run out to check
its windswept perimeter from hour to hour.

GIORGIO
As you do.

JUANA
I have been known to, just to make sure
the circle is still there, unbroken.

GIORGIO
You take a lot of chances for a woman
of your calling.

JUANA
To be a woman is also my calling.

GIORGIO
Then let *me* take a chance.

JUANA
What sort of chance?

GIORGIO
Well, I wonder . . . that is, I . . .

JUANA
What is it? Do you wish to borrow another book?

GIORGIO
Borrow, yes. Not a book exactly.

JUANA
What would you borrow then?

GIORGIO
Christ in Heaven, if only you were a woman.

JUANA
I am a woman.

GIORGIO
No, if you were *only* a woman.
These last days with you here, jabbering
like two parrots in the same tree,
as if we'd waited all our lives to speak,
you've become closer to me than my clothes
—*which you wear.* How long does decency demand
I wait to put an indecent question?

JUANA
Oh, my. You're taking my breath away.

GIORGIO
The question . . .

JUANA
Oh!
   (Covers her mouth with her hands)

GIORGIO
Defending the port? Or keeping your soul in?
Don't look at me as if I were about to abduct you.
I didn't plan this heart's detour either.

18

I don't even know where we are, for pity's sake,
though wherever it is there's an ocean in it,
and us smiling like two porpoises all week.
   (JUANA holds her chest and sits down.)
Are you all right?

JUANA
I don't know. My heart's banging around the walls
of my chest like a falling ball.

GIORGIO
Falling because you dropped it or pushed it?

JUANA
That's what alarms me. At some point,
I had it safely in hand, and then—gone.
   *(He makes as if to kiss her, but does not, as the lights fade.
   When lights come up again, it is a few days later. GIORGIO is
   skipping rocks, while JUANA looks among the shells and vegeta-
   tion.)*

GIORGIO
Well, come on wench, do you want to learn the knack of this or
not?
   (JUANA looks uneasy.)
I shouldn't have said that. It leapt out,
as a gentle tease. I can call you whatever
you like, something more lofty, more neutral.

JUANA
If God knows the source of my love,
I am still a Sister.

GIORGIO
You can also be a flirt. And despite
your strict rule, every inch a woman.
In fact, a few more inches than some.

JUANA
You've gone about taking a poll, have you?

GIORGIO
I suppose I've poled enough in my time.

JUANA
You could tease me, if you must,

with something ancient, perhaps,
from the Latin poets.

GIORGIO
If you've been reading the Latin poets,
you've been ladling round in some very saucy books,
Madam.

JUANA
Purely to improve my Latin, I assure you.
A sterling education is worth the tarnish
of a few obscenities. Though Latin runs high
as the Church, it did begin in the streets.

GIORGIO
Rather specialized vocabulary, wouldn't you say,
gutter Latin?

JUANA
Chasing knowledge, you never know
when you're going to stumble on a randy ancient.

GIORGIO
How about a stumble with a randy youth?
  (She tosses sand at him.)
I suppose you read Propertius and Ovid
and
  (Whispering, as if to pry loose a secret)
. . . Catullus?
  (She nods, hotly embarrassed.)
Oh! God's body, that's good.
To hear him tell it, all of modern Italy
is his heir. Gave a whole new meaning
to the phrase "Latin Quarters." What a lewd cat,
who, if I'm not mistaken, invented the word
for kissing on the lips.

JUANA
"Osculum." But I also read stolid, dignified,
sanctimonious, well-intended,
freshly-laundered, trimly-argued books.
I don't just read those that will set brush-fires
in my limbs. I pick and choose.

GIORGIO
Your library suggests you read everything.
I've known Genoese whores who have slept
with fewer minds.

JUANA
Oh! . . . No, no, I'm not going to take you on.

GIORGIO
You've taken me in, you may as well take me on.

JUANA
Jesus, Joseph, and Mother of God,
you scoundrel! You unchivalrous, low-living,
half-ounce of Italian . . .

GIORGIO
  (Puts a hand over her mouth, holds her)
I adore you. I respect you. I'm in awe of you.
I just don't know how to *be* with you yet.
My etiquette never included . . . well,
for starters, courting a woman dressed like me.
And then there is this minor impediment
of your being a nun. I was raised to kowtow
to anyone wearing the livery of the Church.
Even at carnivals on feast days, when I'd bump
into four-year-olds wearing saints' masks,
I'd genuflect.

JUANA
I confuse you.

GIORGIO
You? No, not your heart, not your mind,
not your faith, not your moods, not your passions.
You don't confuse me. Only the surfaces,
the flounces. Not what I've grown to feel for you
this week, when I should have been at court,
sucking up to the Viceroy like any good,
self-respecting, low-living, half-ounce
of whatever putrefying abomination
you were building up to a moment ago.
There's no confusion about any of that,
just the gloves it carries. Does it ride or walk?
Does it use a cane? Does it bow?

What do I call you in public, in private?
How do I protect your honor from all
the wags, who would be stunned to know anything
so unexalted about you?

JUANA
Pillars of strength must sometimes lie down.

GIORGIO
But only alone. Your adorers, who, I confess,
this whole coast couldn't hold, think of you,
need to think of you, as well-scrubbed, able,
and beyond tempests.

JUANA
You make me sound like a tropic storm
due for mischief at regular intervals.

GIORGIO
I know better than that. I swear, it may
be the only subject that's new to you.

JUANA
That transparent?

GIORGIO
No, no, multi-layered, complex, subtle,
wonderful. But something tells me,
by your modesty, perhaps, *new*.

JUANA
I also never learned to read English.

GIORGIO
Hardly the same . . . Well, maybe the same,
depends on the primer. What's so tempting
about English, I mean as opposed to Chinese,
German, or Arabic (now there's a language
you'd like: a wildflower for your bouquet of tongues).

JUANA
Oh, I'll buy the cartload, if you're peddling.
But with scientists like Harvey, Bacon,
Boyle, Wren, and others, not to mention all
the playwrights and poets, and my dear friend,
Henry Oldenburg, Secretary to the Royal Society,

who acts as my philosophical merchant,
sending me the bound *Transactions* of each meeting,
England is quite the place to be these days.
What an extraordinary paper he just sent me
by a biologist, John Ray, who's convinced
that fossils were not put into rocks by God
as a means to test our faith in Genesis,
but are the remains of creatures that once lived!

GIORGIO
Not a new thought.

JUANA
New here. Sometimes I think the sun would be
new here. But lately I'm more curious
about a Mr. Isaac Newton, who, I'm told,
is doing grand, nimble experiments with light
and gravity, some of which overlap my own.
If he's treading my path into the wilderness,
I'd love to know what Canaans he's come to.
Do you know him?

GIORGIO
I met him once at a dinner at Francesco Redi's
in Florence. A hypnotic speaker.
And his hands moved like an oriental dancer's,
feeling a nonexistent knot on his forehead,
plucking at a pant leg.

JUANA
My English contacts have lost track of him.

GIORGIO
I think it's bad health. I heard he fled
to the country to watch the apples fall.

JUANA
The apples fall?

GIORGIO
That's the joke making the rounds of Italy.
He's become somewhat of a rumor in his own time.

JUANA
What's it like in Turin?

GIORGIO
Majestic. Humbling.

JUANA
No, no, you must tell me so I can see it.

GIORGIO
Ah, so you can see it. Well, then,
you wake up and go to sleep in full view
of the Alps. But I was born higher up,
in Susa, where low clouds look tethered by ropes
of water when it rains, and only in the winter
do the trees seem truly planted: plum-dark shafts
jutting out of the snow, widening
to a flat podium at the bottom.
The winds are all slow dance and rebuff,
and you swear they're pitted with icebergs
when it storms. The mountain pastures
can grow cold and scaly as lizards.
There was always a cataract in the eye
of the lake, which I knew to be ice,
thin, crisp, and largely unwalkable
in early winter, but glorious to play on
a few months later. Even in summer,
the winds would bleat like invisible sheep,
braying and butting and posing in the trees.
Some days I felt footloose among the stars
and the world wasn't big enough for all of me,
and others the slim petiole of a leaf,
spinning turn and turn about, would distract me
all afternoon. In the family graveyard,
the stones were rimmed with ice, like tiny windows,
pane to pane. And always there were
the anatomical mountains, like frozen motion:
plunge, interfold, roll away. I'd watch
how shadows drifted round them, changing light
and contour. At twilight, the sun
was like spilled pollen, soft, palpable,
an émigré crawling along the border of the world.

JUANA
It sounds like a wonderland. Why would you choose
to leave such a place?

GIORGIO
I don't know, the world seemed so plural,
so ripe. I didn't want to miss it
while it was in season.

JUANA
And have you bagged it now, travelling as you do?

GIORGIO
Four valises don't make a life.
You've travelled wider without leaving the province.

JUANA
That may be true. What does it mean, I wonder,
to be able to leave the here-and-now
so easily, with no remorse, just slide across
and set up shop in another time?

GIORGIO
Oh, God, what a thought's buzzing me.
You weren't, you wouldn't . . . you are capable
of it . . . you didn't *lie with me* as a sort of experiment?

JUANA
How could you think such a thing!

GIORGIO
Don't come that maidenly outrage with me.
I'm not chiding, just wondering. Yes or no?

JUANA
Well, it would be a lie to say I wasn't curious,
having known it so often between the sheets
of a book . . . but hardly cold-blooded!
If I wished just to satisfy the body
of my curiosity, I could have done it before this.

GIORGIO
No doubt. You have a vast, invisible army
of murmurers, a kennel of courtiers,
and even adorers in distant capitals
to choose from. Opportunity must have used
a battering ram, not knocked.
I'm amazed you kept your head,
while others about you were losing theirs.

JUANA
My books seemed better suitors:
knew more, borrowed less, made fewer demands.
But surely you were heckled by curiosity, too,
unless you make a habit of habits.

GIORGIO
Very curious, I confess.

JUANA
And what a snare! Hawking down to catch
the honorable Sister Juana Inés in your talons.

GIORGIO
Absolutely. A bragger's dream.
Innkeeper, drinks for all the barnacles
and crayfish! . . . But I also love you,
as far as I can know about such roomy things
in so small a space as a week.
I'd have to be such a dog to trick you.

JUANA
There are many . . .

GIORGIO
There are many who would. Some wilder tribes
like to collect scalps, but it's a sport
that never appealed to me. Anyway,
there isn't much scalp there for a trophy.

JUANA
You *don't* like my short hair.

GIORGIO
It could be longer.
    (Holds up four fingers)
A few fingers' worth? On second thought,
what would the other Sisters think
if you suddenly let it bolt?

JUANA
Perhaps only that I'd grown absent-minded
and unkempt. Poor Sister Juana, such a lamb
of study she hasn't the time to trim her fleece.

26

GIORGIO
The world won't end, if you don't.
Mistress or mistresses, I'll want you either way.

JUANA
You were going to teach me to skip rocks.

GIORGIO
So I was, as thanks for your introducing me
to all the spumoni-colored goblins of your reef.
What a throb of color: like fireworks in mid-air.
And what a clever contraption that boxed window
of yours is! Here I was wondering
what sacred relic you'd brought, swaddled tight.
I should have known. But those gaping eyes
we saw through it—it was like spiraling deep
into Dante's *Inferno.*

JUANA
It will prepare you for all the fish-eyes
and colored scales you'll find at court.
Of course, the women there have satinier skins.
Not all of them, though.

GIORGIO
Meow. You think I wouldn't like a mermaid?
Voluptuous as a siren on top, and the bottom
shimmery Inca gold.

JUANA
Impractical. Not enough woman to love,
and too much fish to fry.

GIORGIO
Find a skipping stone. A wet one is good,
but a mossy one will be too slick.
Look for one about the size of a squashed hummingbird.

JUANA
With or without wings? . . . How's this?

GIORGIO
Good, but see how it cambers on one side?
You'll have to hold it like a bowl,
so it will skid, not cling to the water.

Couch it here in the crook of your finger,
and press it against the fleshy root of your thumb.
That's it. Now the art is to pitch it
flat and low, the first nip close by,
so it will just graze the wave.
(JUANA pitches it, edge down.)

JUANA
Aw, it went down like a rock.

GIORGIO
It *is* a rock.

JUANA
Went down like what it is, then.

GIORGIO
What an outrage. By the way, you tossed it
edgewise. No good at all. That makes it carve
into the muscle of the water. Stoop low,
almost eye to eye with it, and twirl the rock
off your forefinger as you let go.

JUANA
Right. Half-moon of thumb and forefinger.
Crouch. Draw the arm back, and . . . ah!
(Both follow it, counting out loud.)

GIORGIO, JUANA
One, two, three, four, five, six!

GIORGIO
A born skipper.

JUANA
(Saluting)
Aye, aye, sir.
*(GIORGIO continues skipping stones; JUANA sits
and watches him.)*
Seventeen, eighteen . . . Oh! What a rabbit
hopping out to the horizon. It thrills me
all out of proportion to see them jump
like that from one category to another.
A lifeless grey rock suddenly all pitch and flow
and elation and speed, the dead careening
into life. A resurrection of flint.

GIORGIO
When it strikes, perhaps it's like hitting
a palm that lifts gently, then sends it skidding
to the next palm, and so on.

JUANA
Or the angle isn't sharp enough
to pierce the water's skin, just as some spiders
manage to tiptoe across the water
without sinking. How frightening it must be
to be a bug and thirsty, knowing that,
like a man leaning over a cliff to see,
if you lean too far you may topple in and drown.
I'll have to check both when I return
to my labyrinth.

GIORGIO
When must that be?

JUANA
It was supposed to be days ago,
many days ago. And how will you explain
your being so late to the Viceroy's?

GIORGIO
Oh, vandals, highwaymen, minotaurs, pirates,
medusas, Abyssian perverts, duty . . .

JUANA
Duty! Now there's an unlikely thug.

GIORGIO
Overcome as I was by my duty to serve my new host
with the respect and gratitude due him, and,
endeavoring to act with the courtesy and valor
befitting a gentleman, finding myself travelling
at the same time as their renowned and most holy
Sister was planning to undertake her pilgrimage, and
knowing what lawless turns a woman travelling alone
might come to, I naturally felt obliged . . .

JUANA
Out of duty . . .

GIORGIO
. . . out of duty to his highness, and respect for

29

the cloth, to escort the good Sister on her journey,
and, discovering once she had arrived there, that
she meant to return, and would not be dissuaded from
it on any account, her willfulness in such matters
being common knowledge, I naturally felt duty-bound
to ensure her safe return to St. Jerome.

JUANA
You're returning with me?

GIORGIO
Unless you'd rather I didn't.
I could be later, I suppose, but not more truant.
I'll return you home safely, and then I really
must be off.

JUANA
Shall we skip a few more stones before you go?
*(They look for good stones. GIORGIO brings her a small
pile of them.)*
These are all just the right size for me.

GIORGIO
A small token.
(He bows.)

JUANA
A wooing bird never brought his spouse
a sweeter hovel.

GIORGIO
It is a bit bird-like, I admit,
but you warble so sweetly.

JUANA
You like to see me blush.

GIORGIO
And burn. It makes your plumage bright.

JUANA
Let's try some other stuffs, to see
how they skip by comparison.

GIORGIO
Here's a stick, a gull-feather, a shell,
a book . . .

JUANA

Oh, no, no bath for Lucretius, poor soul.

GIORGIO

Why poor, when his thoughts were so well-heeled?

JUANA

Poor Lucretius, his vast troubled life
reduced to this small passage in Suetonius:
(Reads aloud)
"94 B.C., Titus Lucretius, poet, is born. After a love potion had
turned him mad, and he had written, in the intervals of his insan-
ity, several books which Cicero revised, he killed himself by his
own hand in the 44th year of his age."

Imagine, in 54 B.C. he just vanished,
as if a gorgeous, torrential, 44-year-long storm
suddenly stopped. And "by his own hand,"
that's what makes me mad, what chills me.
Giorgio, I don't understand this being
in whose body we dwell like a genie
trapped in a bottle, how one day Lucretius
could wake up feeling lonelier than life.
Faced with tornados, chewing up homes,
with dust-storms ruining crops and everafters,
with floods log-rolling children and art,
with earthquakes pocketing whole cities,
with ordeals by fire, and the Holy Inquisition
    (Crosses herself)
and volcanos frying natives where they lie,
and carnivorous fish like the candiru
or piranha, with drought and dam-burst,
and ghostly diseases that gnaw bone-marrrow,
or cripple, or craze—faced with such
rampant miseries and ordeals that need no
special bidding, but come freely, giving
their horror like alms, you'd think human beings
would cling to their breath, glisten with rage,
hold out against the rot that unmixes,
not chew on their bowels like a shark,
not wish to die swiftly like any insect or fawn.
Death does such fine work without us.
And Lucretius, a man of poise and vision,

for whom all the far-flung treats of being
fitted easily into the cellars of his heart,
he wakes up one day, lonelier than life,
and takes death in like a bucket of milk.

GIORGIO
You ache for him.

JUANA
That poor man, how he must have suffered.

GIORGIO
I swear, you would have called him "Titus"
and skipped stones with him. He lives for you.

JUANA
When I think of a mind like that,
so well-stocked and full of humor,
like a homestead staked out against the elements,
then the centuries seem only a small fog
on a brisk morning. By afternoon,
it will lift, and all will be clear.

GIORGIO
That would have to be quite an afternoon.

JUANA
It was on the *afternoon* of the Sixth Day
that God created man.

GIORGIO
And ever since that man's been returning
the compliment.

JUANA
You're not one of those Baconian atheists?

GIORGIO
A hog of pure reason? No, for all
the panic and joy it gives me,
there's more between my cells than blood.
   (Finds an apple in his sack)
Would you consider skipping an apple?
In honor of Mr. Newton.

JUANA
Absolutely. How about that dead bird we found

yesterday?

GIORGIO
You want me to skip a dead bird?

JUANA
Well, it would be both larger and bulkier
than what we have here, but lighter.
Be game; let's try it.

GIORGIO
All right, I'm willing. Where was it?

JUANA
I think it was under that skirt of rock
just beyond the sand-spit, where the sea-grapes
are twisted around a shift of sand-dune.

GIORGIO
You should have been a map-maker.

JUANA
A scavenger doesn't forget the best
places to dine.
(They climb over the rocks, to look for the bird.)

CURTAIN

ACT I, Scene 3

Sister JUANA's cell. She sits at her desk, composing a poem, while NUNS bustle in and out. MARÍA enters with an armload of letters and gifts, putting them on the table.

JUANA
Not more gifts!

MARÍA
They arrive every day, Sister, like stray cats.
For your birthday next month mainly,
but also for the feast of St. Stephen's,
for Ramadan, for the winter solstice even . . .

JUANA
   (Laughs)
I see: any day's a holiday for the giver.
We'll scatter them to the other sisters
and the poor. Keep a tally of each letter
and what was sent, and I'll write a verse
or two in reply.

MARÍA
What care you take, to answer them in verses.

JUANA
I think in verses, I dream in verses,
I will probably die in verses.
Others gabble dialect; I gabble verses.
But they're mostly trifles baked without recipe
on the heat of a momentary whim. That's all.

MARÍA
That you intend so little by them
makes them all the more remarkable,
as those six gentleman said
by joint letter yesterday.

JUANA
Bah!
They'd like to think it's a holy relic
to be eulogized, not a frame for my greetings,
or a crutch for lame logic, or a mental knick-knack
tied up with a bow to amuse a sick friend.
What a cloudburst of praise; and how embarrassing.

34

The poems they refer to were modest,
occasional verses. They wish to think more of *me,*
and think more of *them.* I've just answered
with this doggerel, which even they will see
is doggerel, a leash for my thoughts.
    (Hands it to her. MARÍA reads it to herself.)

MARÍA
They'll find its metal gleaming, as I do.

JUANA
Shame on you. I'll have to give you
better poets to read.
    (Picks up a sheet of paper)
Here is gleaming verse. It's by an Englishman
now dead, alas, William Habington.
And what I've gone through just to hold
this single layer of his thoughts.
I learned of it from a Swiss,
who had it from a Frenchman, who translated it
on request, and sent it here by sea.
But even having changed its clothes twice
and gone a voyage, it's so fresh and lively.
Listen to this:
    (Reads aloud)

When I survey the bright
    Celestial sphere:
So rich with jewels hung, that night
Doth like an Aethiop bride appear,

My soul her wings doth spread
    And heaven-ward flies,
Th'Almighty's mysteries to read
In the large volume of the skies.

MARÍA
Oh!

JUANA
    (Handing her the poem)
Here, have a read.

MARÍA
    (Reading it to herself)

Oh, this is beautiful.
(She reads the last two stanzas aloud:)

Thus those Celestial fires,
Though seeming mute,
The fallacy of our desires
And all the pride of life confute.

For they have watched since first
The world had birth:
And found sin in itself accurst
And nothing permanent on earth.
(MARÍA exhales loudly.)

JUANA
Your breath leaves you. I've read it
a hundred times since it arrived, and each time
my flesh crawls like a sphinx to meet it.
The eye moves so nimbly. The scope is so vast.
It makes every cell crane, to see the skies
farther, to see the world deeper.
(NUNS, coming and going, arrange chairs and
other furniture.)

FIRST NUN
Will this do, Sister? And perhaps this one,
being better stuffed, for the Viceroy?

JUANA
Yes, fine. María, see to it, would you?

SECOND NUN
The menu, Sister. Besides your *jicarandas,*
there's a sort of orange and cinnamon lather;
the recipe's from my cousin in the convent
of St. Catherine of Sienna.

JUANA
Sounds good. Make a few extras, would you?
We're due a visit by Father Marceno,
who is sure to be bothered by something.
I think the fly buzzing him at the moment
is a sermon by a Portuguese Jesuit.
Quite an old argument, it only just surfaced here
in a pretty book of his essays.

FIRST NUN
You've read it then?

JUANA
Oh, I have, and it couldn't be more ably argued.
What an orator! Once he traps you
in the swift chains of his logic,
there's no squirming out.
A fine mind, if a too smug one.

FIRST NUN
(To SECOND NUN)
Sounds like there could be a small conflagration.
Make sure there's plenty of drink to quench it.

SECOND NUN
I will.

JUANA
María, what are you up to?

MARÍA
Just fixing these horsetails, Sister.

JUANA
Trot over here a moment with them.
(Aside to MARÍA)
My Lord of Turin knows to come
this evening with the others?

MARÍA
(Whispering)
Yes, Madam, both he and his servant.
Shall I arrange anything special for him?

JUANA
No, no, let him sort himself out.
I'd rather not arrange him,
nor be in the mind that would wish to
arrange him. Fetch the lute;
let's practice that song of yours.

(Lights dim. When the lights come on, it is evening and candles are burning in Sister Juana's cell. Vespers have just finished. A crowd returns to her room, chatting noisily as they enter. Various NUNS, MOTHER SUPERIOR, the VICEROY and his WIFE,

COURTIERS, MARÍA, GIORGIO and RICARDO, MEN dressed in foreign costumes, SERVANTS. JUANA and FATHER MAR-CENO are heatedly discussing something.)

VICEROY
Sister Juana, please, you two have been quibbling
like druids since Vespers. Include us,
and I will kiss your hem, if I may.

JUANA
Viceroy, forgive me. It concerns a sermon
by Padre Antonio Vieyra, which is this season's
fashion in all the diocese. Father Marceno
has been ardently pressing me to assay it,
which, as I am no lapidary mind, I am loath to.

FATHER MARCENO
True enough, she's nearly argued me
out of an answer, but as I know her mastery
with such issues, I am on the verge,
the precipice, let us say the edge of,
in a word, scrimping her objections
with an overriding plea, that is a formal request . . .

JUANA
As you've ordered me to do so, I will,
but find it doubly difficult, not just
to overturn such deft arguments
on so complicated a theme, but because
I dislike impugning anyone. I will do it,
but only because my objections are eased
by knowing we will be the sole witness,
and your command excuses an error
that to other eyes might seem presumptuous
in a sex so unfit for the subject of letters.
. . . I do dread having to say off the cuff
what I would otherwise pause to think about,
but here is my understanding of his premise,
and my response:
    He speaks of the great goodness of Christ
toward the end of his life, citing the judgment
of three Holy Fathers, St. Augustine, St. Thomas,
and St. Chrysostom. St. Augustine felt

that Christ's greatest goodness was to die.
However, our orator argues it was much greater
of Christ to absent Himself than to die.
He substantiates this by saying that Christ
loved men more than His life since He gave it
for them. He develops this logic
by noting that Christ made no demonstration
of sorrow while dying on the Cross,
although he did make such a one in the Garden,
precisely because He was to depart,
for He was far more sensible
of His approaching absence than of His death.
An additonal proof, he says, is that
though Christ died once and absented Himself
once, for death he had but one remedy—
resurrection. But for his absence He had
an infinite number of remedies
through his Sacramental Presence.
Thus, so much more does Christ feel His absence
than His death that He subjects Himself
to perpetual death in order not to suffer
a moment's absence. Therefore, it was
a greater act to absent Himself than to die.

*(Though JUANA continues her summary of Vieyra's sermon,
she cannot be heard. Instead, the audience hears a conversation
among some courtiers upstage.)*

FIRST COURTIER
And she says she has only passing knowledge
of the text.

SECOND COURTIER
Must have grabbed quite an eyeful
as the coach reeled past.

THIRD COURTIER
Remind me not to drop any love letters
in her presence.
(Shows a letter under his tunic)

FIRST COURTIER
What's that? Give us a look.
(They read the letter.)

SECOND COURTIER
Oh, so you've got Helena between the legs
of your compass.

FIRST COURTIER
I thought the sands of her hourglass figure
had just about run out.

SECOND COURTIER
Her father's dowry for her hasn't though.
An unusual looking girl to have so many suitors.

THIRD COURTIER
Let's just say, I know where my bread is buttered.

FIRST COURTIER
On the crust of a compliment, by the looks
of this letter. Happy hunting my friend.
Remember us when you're in the luxury of her lap.
   *(The sounds of their laughing and joking fade, as JUANA's
voice gets louder.)*

JUANA
These are the sermon's main reasons and proofs,
which, not to be too lengthy, I've abridged
and glued to the clumsiness of my own style,
through which they undoubtedly lose
a great deal of color, force, and vehemence.

FATHER MORENO
Not at all. Most fair. A fine rendering
of his argument, and, I might add, served up
so flavorfully, I'm once again nourished
by it. But you are not, I wager.

JUANA
No. If I *must* debate the matter,
I agree with St. Augustine, that Christ's gift
was not to absent Himself but to die.
This goes without saying, really,
for what a man most treasures is life
and honor, and Christ sacrificed both
in His ignominious death. As God,
He had already granted man the great marvels
of creation and preservation; but, as man,

there was nothing more to give but His life.
Since He is the only one able to judge
His own acts, it's clear that, had there been
a greater act, He would have said so.
Therefore, it was his greatest mercy.
What sorrow is there in absence,
but that of being deprived of the sight
of the beloved?
    (Catches Giorgio's eye)
Death is a more particularized thing,
for while absence brings a limited lack,
death brings a perpetual lack.
Thus death is a greater pain than absence,
because it is a greater absence.
    (JUANA'S voice fades into the background and cannot be heard
by the audience, whose attention is drawn to the SERVANTS up-
stage, who squat and lean, joking and talking.)

FIRST SERVANT
It's too fiddly for me,
all the buttoning and unbuttoning,
all the what-fors and wherefores.
If the shirt fits, it's buttoned well enough,
I says.

SECOND SERVANT
That's clear from the buttoned fit y'er wearin'.

FIRST SERVANT
And you'd think the Viceroy'd have enough
on his plate, with him barely in office,
and already he's lost two ships to pirates,
the Indians are puttin' the prickle on 'im
at every turn, the crops are poor enough
to litter pups in, and the Archbishop
lowing like an unmilked cow about all
the calf-eyes and parties at the convents.

THIRD SERVANT
I hear there's a new Viceregal in the stars, too.

FIRST SERVANT
You wouldn't think he'd be weavin'
theological straw when the whole stable

could go up, poof!, at any second.
(RICARDO joins them.)
Here, now,
you're the new one from the boot, aren't you?

RICARDO
Closer to the ankle: Turin.
(A NUN passes around a tray of exotic, shimmery pastries.)

FIRST SERVANT
Try some of that brown froth there.
It's like waking up inside an angel's stomach.
They compete, you know, from convent to convent.
Chocolate with cinnamon pearls on top,
dried apricots soaked in rum,
chocolate saucers with chocolate clouds
floating in 'em and just a drizzle of vanilla
layin' across it, lamb ribs drippin' with fat
and mint, and spicy meats that can cave in
the side of your face.

THIRD SERVANT
Not for me, lads! I'd end up ringing the bell
for Matins without ever leaving bed.

FIRST SERVANT
Oh, it's a lark being a gentleman's man
at court here. Got to watch yourself though,
be smooth and gentile in front of the Sisters.
Ralph here, he likes the dumb show better
than the food; but not me, I'm no dandy.
I figure asses were made for scratchin'.
I got an ass; I scratch it.
*(MOTHER SUPERIOR overhears his last line, and looks
at him, wide-eyed.)*

FIRST SERVANT
. . . to cajole it into carrying a heavier load,
Sister. You can also use a carrot on a stick,
so as to lead it on. Beast of burden,
you know, the ass.

MOTHER SUPERIOR
And so dependable.

FIRST SERVANT
Oh, yes, dependable, that it is.

MOTHER SUPERIOR
Not a profound or intelligent beast.

FIRST SERVANT
No, no, not profound.

MOTHER SUPERIOR
But well-designed for its lot in life.

FIRST SERVANT
Perform whole days without working up a sweat.

MOTHER SUPERIOR
And they have such sensitive faces.
To look into one sincerely is to understand the world.

FIRST SERVANT
Ain't it the truth.
  (MOTHER SUPERIOR joins the other group, where JUANA's talking becomes audible again.)

JUANA
The one absent suffers only through not seeing
the beloved, but neither one is injured.
So death is a greater grief than absence,
since absence is just that; while death is death
and and absence. Thus if you consider
all it includes, it will be a greater grief.
So for Christ to die was His greatest act of mercy.

VICEROY
Well done, well done. You've left him slain
in the catacombs of his logic.

FATHER MARCENO
And me so well persuaded I wonder
if I may try the limits of your generosity,
if you would deign to jot down these thoughts
at your leisure. Nothing fancy, a few
casual ideas, some idle ruminations
will do. I'll take no modest *no* for an answer.

JUANA
Provided it's for your eyes alone.
Were it meant to travel wider,
I'd have to dress it more carefully.

FATHER MARCENO
For my eyes solely, just as you say,
to aid my devotions. Nothing fancy.

JUANA
I'm quite exhausted. Do let's have some food
and music now.

VICEROY
Well earned. Sister, bring some of those
whipped cyclones over there, would you?
(A NUN brings a tray of confections.)

FIRST GENTLEMAN
Sister, that verse play of yours
last week was so elegant and full of veils
I'd hoped you'd have another one tonight,
a confection as heavenly as this.
(Pops a cake into his mouth)

JUANA
The week's duties left us no time,
I'm afraid. There was that quake at Tampico,
you may recall, which split the earth the width
of two confessionals. We had all on
to tell the living from the dead, since both
were breathless and transfigured by shock,
and the horror of their ploughed land
turning *them* under like crops. It nearly
sealed their faith in the supernatural.

FIRST GENTLEMAN
The supernatural goodness of you Sisters
seals *our* faith.

JUANA
You mean we keep your wayward conscience
from spooking you at night.

SECOND GENTLEMAN
He deserved that, frivolous pup.
He only walks abroad at night to check
the lay of the land.

SECOND COURTIER
 (To THIRD COURTIER)
I believe your Helena is being mentioned again.

JUANA
However, we have rehearsed a small song,
as his lordship bade us last week.

VICEROY
So I did. I asked you for a popular aire.
Love and heartbreak, melancholy and confusion.
That sort of thing.

JUANA
The sum I shall never figure, my Lord,
is why you men prefer your poetry
exalted, and your songs down to earth.

VICEROY
 (Laughs)
Nor is it fitting we tell you.
 (MARÍA sings a short, Elizabethan love song. Applause)

JUANA
Beautiful, María.
A voice like a desert bird.
 (Others agree.)
Come, Sister Magdalena, the real musician,
play something.
 (Hands her the lute; while MAGDALENA plays a tune, the servants' conversation becomes louder upstage.)

FIRST SERVANT
Now I've got a song a bit closer to the bones,
if you get my drift. I heard it off a bloke
at the Crow's Neck the other night,
chap up from the docks. It pretends
to be a song sung by the ocean current
off the point of Yucatan. She's a lady
current, see. Goes like this:

(Sings)
Come ride the fish-bright
  swells of my flesh
and lay by in my limbs,
  greener than a glade.
Run aground, sailor,
  in my dark, wooded eyes,
swing round your mizzen,
  shipwreck in my thighs.

Only come to my harbor;
  sweet is the port air.
Time will drop its sail
  like a ketch in a lagoon.

There's a berth in my hips
  As wide as the moon,
a ribcage roomier than the sea,
  and here, awash
between outcry and the deep blue,
  my sinking heart
will fathom life from you.

SECOND SERVANT
Now there's a current would make me take the plunge.

FIRST SERVANT
With a woman at home as good-looking
as your Louisa?
  (To RICARDO, whispering)
He's got a wife you could slice bread with!

VICEROY
  (To GIORGIO)
Homesick for your eyrie in the snow?
Man to man, doesn't it dampen the drive,
all that ice?

GIORGIO
Wouldn't be much nation left, if it did.
I think you'd find the snow
merely cleansed the palate,
like a tart water-ice after a robust meal.

VICEROY

Well, you're welcome to our balmy outpost.
It can be a rugged go here at times,
but, as you see, also a very pleasant one.
(Toasts him)
May you find the larder always packed,
the weather always mild, the chase for game
always hearty, and the hospitality
of our good Sisters, without whom we would die
of boredom in our palatial ruts,
always in season.

GIORGIO

(Returns the toast)
And the Viceroy always so gracious.

VICEROY

That most of all.

CURTAIN

ACT II, Scene 1

Some months later, in GIORGIO's chamber at the Viceroy's court. He sits daydreaming. RICARDO enters.

RICARDO
My Lord, a messenger from the convent
of St. Jerome brought this letter.

GIORGIO
(Takes the envelope)
What's this?
(Reads it and laughs)
So, in her agile thoughts, we're together, too.
There must be four of us then.
It's a sonnet: a rose-bush
with fourteen blood-red flowers,
in which she speaks to my mirage in her cell.
How like her: modest, yet daring.
(Hands it to RICARDO, who reads it)

RICARDO
Very pretty, my Lord.

GIORGIO
Ah, Ricardo, what a troupe of weeks
has come parading through my life,
each more dizzying and acrobatic
than the last. A regatta of days,
full of walks and rides and books
and quiet, illuminated hours
during which we've talked of nearly nothing,
nearly everything. Even her idle chatter
has sunlit ways. Dear God, my wishes
are like homing pigeons; if only
I could shed the miles right now.
What's a day? A few hours
strapped together by the sun;
she makes mine glide like a pendulum,
dividing and uniting in a stroke,
each moment meeting its double on the run,
till gravity pulls it back again.
And yet I lie. Time doesn't move at all,
it stammers, it gags, it hiccups, it faints,

it throws tantrums, it sleeps till noon.
Time and I are like two ghouls
locked in the coliseum of these walls.
First, it whips me with its long, moaning hours
in which a minute is a multitude
and nothing can split the armor of a day.
And then I snake its wrist
by nimbly picturing her: the spa
of her glance, her wit a whetstone
that sharpens itself, her long fluent fingers
like the legs of a spider carved out of topaz.
I think of her dressing in the morning,
when the dew is a flat cloud on the grass,
and make the moment last longer
than her dressing does!
Clothed in the soft linen of her books,
her old underlinens gone to ragmen
who will sell them to be pulped
for new books, she is where the books
begin and end. A yet unborn one,
as she sleeps, may hold
her end in its lap. Lucky linen,
to have such a muse at hand.

    Ricardo, be off a moment.
I've a letter to write,
and will call you back for it.
    (RICARDO leaves; GIORGIO takes out a sheet of paper.)
And now, to be safe, what shall I say?
It must work like litmus:
be written in pink, and read in blue.
    (Writes, and says aloud)
Dearest . . . Sister
. . . All that keeps me from you,
and the rest of my beloved family,
will I'm afraid detain me here at court another week.
For such is the habit of our diplomacy
that, like a spark on the plains of Africa,
it must be kept discrete in a small span,
lest it be quenched by all the wet weathers
of the world that combine for malice
when a bold spirit blazes. Stroll with me
in a book, whose vellum is the sail *Vela*

in the night sky, whose vellum is my flesh.
On the round map of your world,
I've laid my lines, and will return to you
next week, hand over hand if need be,
as I am,
Your loving brother,
Giorgio
(Blots letter, folds, and seals it)
Oh for a French postman.
Ricardo!
(RICARDO enters.)

RICARDO
My Lord.

GIORGIO
Carry this, you know where, to my fine Sister.
And, for God's sake, be unobserved.

RICARDO
I shall, my Lord, just as you ask.
You waste no trust on me.
A Holy Father waits below.

GIORGIO
A tall man, with a permanent storm on his face?

RICARDO
(Laughs)
Yes!

GIORGIO
Father Suárez. Send him up.
(RICARDO tucks the letter inside his tunic and leaves. A clergyman enters. As GIORGIO described, his face is ominous and stern.)

FATHER SUÁREZ
My Lord of Turin.

GIORGIO
Holy Father, won't you sit down
and drink a cordial wine with me,
since it's most cordial
of you to honor me with a visit.

I know you by your calling
to be an apt and efficient man
of the Church.

FATHER SUÁREZ
My "calling" as you say . . .
Yes, I've heard they call me the Bishop's "scythe."
It does me no offense, since my work
for the Bishop is somewhat like a scythe:
I harvest ripe souls, and weed out
those that choke the patch.
I'll take the cordial,
    (Takes a glass from GIORGIO and sips)
but it's on that very business I come.

GIORGIO
I'm merely a courtier, a foreigner as well;
how can I repay your interest?

FATHER SUÁREZ
First, there is no man foreign to God,
only good men and evil men, good women
and evil women. To be brief,
for some time now we've heard rumors
about Sister Juana Inés de la Cruz,
the Holy Sister at the Convent of St. Jerome.
. . . You will not deny that you know her . . .

GIORGIO
I have had the pleasure.

FATHER SUÁREZ
That, instead of pursuing a mum, pristine life,
delivering herself to penance, liturgy,
and her God, she willfully deals
in *philosophy,* theological debate, and science,
dares to write treatises which consider
Church doctrine, and, worst of all, scribbles
poetry and plays, those of which celebrate
the Holy Mother Church in lofty spirit
and balanced language, naturally we welcome
and applaud, but those which gabble
and keep shop with profaner goods
unbecome a church sister to have any commerce with,

indeed, would unbecome a genteel maiden.
It is gross wantonness that in her chambers
she would entertain such thoughts,
let alone raise them up, and clothe them in words.
Further, that she blights the younger nuns
by her example, instructing them,
as I have heard, in such studies as *Logic, Physics,
Mathematics,* and the *Stars.* Further,
that instead of living modestly, by prayer
and good works, that she stages all manner
of experiments in her rooms, receives messengers
from abroad and, like queen of the vestibule,
is paid court to by all the great minds
of Europe, who come to her railing
before the Viceroy's! Outrage to both Church
and Crown. If she has a mind to . . .

GIORGIO
She has a mind like a needle, Father,
that enters a subject, probes deep
into its every whorl and layer,
and withdraws even sharper and brighter than before.

FATHER SUÁREZ
Then you don't deny her wild actions?

GIORGIO
To what purpose deny what you obviously know?

FATHER SUÁREZ
I know that she's a cavilling bird!

GIORGIO
In Rome, I've heard cardinals cavil worse over less.

FATHER SUÁREZ
Mind what *you* say!

GIORGIO
She is so *alive.* God, who filled the world
with wonders, filled her with a passion
to know them all.
    (Aside)
He has not seen her. What a thirst to read

52

consumes her! She will not be ignorant.
She studies all the time, and heaven forbid
there are not books at hand. She can't settle
unless she learns something somehow:
she'll examine the bare beams of a ceiling
to see why they appear to converge and go down
as they recede; she'll fry one egg in oil
and another in syrup, to learn how one unites
and the other breaks up; she'll put sifted flour
under a spinning top to observe its spiral path;
or she'll consider the variety of odd characters
who may share one human being's nature.
In her library, she's life's keenest borrower.
    (To FATHER SUÁREZ)
Scout the province,
you'll find no greater celebrant of God,
the world's architect and provider.
If you condemn her because she is eager
for knowledge, if her real crime is to love life,
then what have we come to?

FATHER SUÁREZ
We have come to heresy,
for it's not in Heaven alone that salvation lies,
not in the soughing of crooked breaths,
nor is world of any lasting consequence
except that it contribute to the one
word of God. Her eyes should be kneading
life's varied grains into a single dough,
and the yeast of her devotion
giving it archways and spires within.
In any case, she was once a lady of the court,
a lay sister, and if what she felt
was not consonant with the language
of church life (as it was not),
then she ought not to have chosen a cloister,
but a husband.

GIORGIO
What wife do you know whose husband
would permit her to study?

FATHER SUÁREZ
And rightly so! Because you are foreign,
I'll grant the rules of our society
may not be fully known to you,
but, by God and the Church, the laws of nature are!
That a maiden should be married to study
is unseemly, unnatural, undignified, and unchristian.

GIORGIO
As I recall, St. Jerome said that women
should not preach, but *not* that they might not learn.

FATHER SUÁREZ
It's not her learning, but *what* she learns
that offends, just as it is right and fine
to speak with God's gift of voice, but not to blaspheme.
In any case, there are far worse charges.

GIORGIO
Such as?

FATHER SUÁREZ
She is known to consort, like a common woman,
with a certain courtier . . .

GIORGIO
Father . . .

FATHER SUÁREZ
  (Pulls out a piece of paper, consults it)
You were *observed,* on the 5th of August,
in the year of our Lord, 1687, at the ocean
near Veracruz, climbing over the reef
in a manner wholly unbefitting a nun,
and you were observed, shall we say,
to be altering her habits . . .
I'll regale you with no more charges just now.
Enough you know how thick the case is against her.

GIORGIO
  (Under his breath)
Like quicksand.

FATHER SUÁREZ
I come to the meat of my visit.

GIORGIO
If all that was appetizer,
I doubt I'll have the stomach for it.

FATHER SUÁREZ
I wager you will. I've come to suggest
an unusual treaty, which might suit us both:
that she leave the convent at once,
break her vows with the Church,
and vanish with you, *provided* you take her
far away beyond trouble, to your country perhaps,
and there lead a quiet, if not a decent, life,
in which at all costs there will be an end
to writing, teaching, and dallying with doctrine.
I need not tell you, I trust, what a rare chance
I offer her.

GIORGIO
Indeed.

FATHER SUÁREZ
The wide bosom of the Church
knows no bounds, but on such matters as heresy
the answer is swift, blunt, and clear.
I have it in my calling to "scythe" her,
and would, were not the Bishop against it.
To speak plainly, because she is no anonymous
defiler, but respected by many,
and swiftly becoming an example to other maidens
who lust after learning, that she not,
at all costs, be turned into a martyr,
and thus, in her punishment, cause worse evil
by inspiring others to forfeit their almighty souls.

GIORGIO
Your offer is most generous.
I will discuss it with her.

FATHER SUÁREZ
Mind that if you agree to these terms,
you leave by night, like common villains,
for so you are. No one may spite the Church
by day, especially a woman.
It defies God's law, and all the laws of society.

Good day, my Lord.

GIORGIO
Holy Father.
(FATHER SUÁREZ leaves.)
So, I must marry my Sister.
Ricardo! Ah, I'd forgotten,
he's already off.

RICARDO
No, my Lord, I've not left yet.
I thought it best to wait.
And heard what passed between you:
a sour business, that. Will it worsen
or fade of its own accord, do you think?

GIORGIO
I don't know. She has friends in high places.
Still, no place is higher than the Church.
Even its low cards can outstrip aces
and make fretwork of kings. Stay a moment,
you'll carry a different letter.
(Sits and begins writing)

RICARDO
The letter is safe with me, my Lord,
provided I am safe.

GIORGIO
Just so. I'd better go myself.

CURTAIN

ACT II, Scene 2

A few days later, at the convent. Morning. JUANA holds a large ball.

JUANA
María, come see this ball Giorgio has brought me.
It's from Turin.

MARÍA
Is it for a game?

JUANA
More for a combat, it would seem, than a game.
As he explained it to me, though there was
much to digest, facing each other
on a windswept field stand two groups
of eleven men each side: four brazen ones,
"forwards" he said (though they could not be
more forward than Giorgio), who punish the ball
when it gets near the net; then three men
who have only a back and a half between them;
and lastly four men with complete backs
who sweep the mess . . .

MARÍA
What mess?

JUANA
I'm not sure. But truly, it doesn't matter.
The key thing is the teams fight over the ball,
debate it with their legs, this way,
that way, snatching it, pawing it, until
one team runs it clear, hazing it downfield
from player to player, as if they were
a tribe chasing quarry into a net.
A sort of hunting game, I think.

MARÍA
And while the first players are chasing the ball
into the net?

JUANA
The others lap at their hocks like hyenas
and try to steal it away.

MARÍA
How awful!

JUANA
Well, perhaps I didn't follow it clearly.
Maybe there's a litle less ruckus.
Although, I have it on good authority
from a peripatetic son of a Persian ambassador
that Asians play a game called "polo,"
in which horsemen bash about an enemy's skull.
At least in *this* game the ball is no relative
whose wits are still jelly.

MARÍA
Oh, how gruesome!

JUANA
Come on, now, María, let's give it a try.
  (She bounces the ball.)

MARÍA
Ugh.
  (Looks nauseated)
I couldn't.
I swear I'll be sick.

JUANA
Oh, piffle, María, join the living.
I think the knack is to skip with it.
Yes, I think that's what he did.
  (She skip-dribbles a few steps, tapping the ball ahead.)
Like that! *Ah!* And, apparently,
you may also hit it soundly with your head.
  (She tosses it up, crosses herself, and shakily bounces it off her head, off-stage.)

GIORGIO
  (Enters, carrying the ball)
Well done, Sister Juana,
I'll make a Turin of you yet!
  (María runs out, demurely.)

JUANA
Did you find it comfortable,

sleeping in my cell?

GIORGIO
You know I did.
  (Kisses her)
And I thought when I crossed the sea
I'd have monsters to wrestle with.

JUANA
I've often enough seen a dragon
rolling in your lap.

GIORGIO
Merely a unicorn escaped
from the tapestry of my soul.

JUANA
  (Picks up a hand-mirror)
Shall I pose with a mirror, then?

GIORGIO
. . . Will you marry me?

JUANA
Marry you?

GIORGIO
Marry me. Abandon the whole flock
of your crowblack habits,
soap off the ring, and replace it
with mine. Though a holy woman,
you are hardly wedded to the Church.
In more exact observation,
you're a woman wedded, repeatedly, to me.

JUANA
I am a woman most often wedded to her will.

GIORGIO
And your will wedded to curiosity.
Imagine, courting a woman with news!
If I bring you a flower, you're likely
to dissect it! For you, the unknown
is like a fugue which books and senses
teach you note by note, but without

your ever losing the sound of the melody.
I love you for it. And will petition that.
All the wounds of the world
into which you'd like to peer
with the affectionate curiosity
of a surgeon: you could see them with me,
travelling the world; enjoying over coffee
those distant friends you're doomed here
to greet only in letters;
and learning letters at schools,
which here you're doomed only to read of
over coffee; with kindred spirits
to sustain you and miles to protect you.

JUANA
Protect me? Am I in danger?
Tell me, what's at work?

GIORGIO
Father Suárez paid me a call,
with quite a tale of their spying on you.

JUANA
No! What an outrage!

GIORGIO
His report's a diary of our doings;
your riding horses at Cuernavaca
seems especially to have titillated them.

JUANA
Imagine! He sends his spies to watch me
hoisting the black sails of my habit.

GIORGIO
Listen to this: rather than acting now
and do Heaven-knows-what mischief to you,
thus letting you prove an example,
they offer us the out of eloping together.
    (JUANA is so surprised she sits down.)

JUANA
Never! I'll stay and fight.

GIORGIO
No, no, this is not a matter for pride.

60

This is serious as death,
for unless my account is in arrears,
they have the means, and will, to break you.
Let's go while there's a chance.

JUANA
And my students? Who would train their minds,
which I've cleared from weedways
and there planted up such thoughts
as will ripen, I hope, into full heads of grain.
How could I leave them now?

GIORGIO
They'll carry on by themselves.

JUANA
But if you're afraid such a granite force
will crush me, picture what it will do to them.
Their eyes, so inquisitive and fresh,
will be lifeless as those on marble statues,
which seem the perfect epitome
of beauty, until you realize that in them
you can see nothing but stone.
If I give in, so will the others.
The Bishop is right to be afraid of my example.
He should be afraid of his own as well;
let him act a devil, and they'll call him one.
But to leave with you . . . it is appealing.
Let me think it through.
I know you must hurry back to court,
which is a grim penance:
it rends my fabric so when you go.

GIORGIO
I thought it best to trust this news
to no letter, and came at once last night,
but I must return before they notice.
The week will seem like seven cities
to be conquered, house by house,
gutter by gutter, rat by rat.

JUANA
Flea by flea?

GIORGIO
Mote by mote. Atom by atom.

JUANA
Thank you, my Democritus.
I should go with you, if only
to prevent such carnage.

GIORGIO
You could marry me . . .

JUANA
I'll tell you soon, when I've considered
the ripples of this new wave.
But my instinct is to fight,
to gamble for it all.

GIORGIO
You could persuade me
to build back the walls of Jericho.

JUANA
Giorgio, until I see you next.
Until then, my world will be eclipsed.

CURTAIN

ACT III, Scene 3

Sister Juana's cell. She is painting at an easel. On the table is a bowl of peonies or other lush, exotic flowers; parts of them, dissected, lie beside an antique microscope. Other antique devices. NUNS come in casually and go, delivering things, borrowing books, inquiring about things. A NUN carrying a large pot of what could be stew bustles in. JUANA tastes the stew, thinks a moment, then goes to a shelf and takes down a bottle. She spills some into it. They stir it and taste, approve. The cook leaves, and JUANA returns to her painting. MARÍA enters with a handful of papers.

JUANA
Good morning, María.

MARÍA
Good morning, Sister.

JUANA
What news today? Does the world dawn as usual?
Hand me that maul-stick, would you?
   (MARÍA hands JUANA a leather strap and stick that painters use to steady their hands.)
It's so hard to do peonies.

MARÍA
The mountains?

JUANA
The flowers . . . the mountains would be hard, too.

MARÍA
   (Consulting her handful of papers)
There's an ornate gentleman waiting to see you;
I believe he's come with those instruments you wanted.

JUANA
Astrolabes. And one of Dr. Boyle's barometers
for keeping a history of the weather.

MARÍA
I've sent him to the kitchen
to have some breakfast.

JUANA
Good.

MARÍA
A note from his excellency,
Señor Cabrera, who wishes to call,
with a view to persuading you to pose
for a portrait.

JUANA
Lovely. I so admire his work.
You know when you peel a lemon,
how, pulling back the skin, beads of scent
jump up and tang the nose?
His paintings are like that for the eyes.

MARÍA
And these two, just arrived,
which I've not yet had chance to scan.

JUANA
Leave them there.
    (Motions to a basket)

MARÍA
    (Glancing over JUANA's shoulder)
Sister, watching you paint reminds me
of something that lately I've been wondering . . .

JUANA
Yes?

MARÍA
Do you recall, some time ago,
when we were discussing "inertia"?

JUANA
Mmm.

MARÍA
It seemed, then, that you thought
matter to be inspiring, but not inspired itself.

JUANA
Well put.

MARÍA
I've been thinking, then, that one
couldn't really love science and beauty

both, perhaps; for, though science is knowledge,
and it is possible to love knowledge,
and beauty is given godliness,
and it is impossible not to love
the gifts of God, it would seem the more
one delved into the details of matter
the less beautiful it would be, or rather,
the less "beauty" would enter the picture at all.

JUANA
   (Stops painting)
Just the opposite.
Since we're bound by the laws of Nature—
the sun that shines the same on everyone,
good, wicked, fat, just, deranged, ambidextrous,
the sun that invigorates grasses and crops
on which cows feed (and you, fortunate
to be at the top of your food chain,
come feeding on the cow) and, underground,
causes lean stirrings in the bulb;
the force of Gravity; all the weatherworks—
bound in this way, we are all slaves of matter.
That maul-stick I asked you for
moments ago, to have it one of us
was obliged to lift it up and bring it here.
The terrain between a wish and its fulfillment
may be vast as the tundra.
We are all run by blind forces at work
in the world: the marrying itch, the sap flow.
We are like a prism, under whose sheer face
lie all the orderly colors of life,
if only we could shine a light clear through
and know them. You're right,
they're quite indifferent to our aspirations,
to sanctity, mercy, decency, justice.
And yet, they are not indifferent.
If ever there was a good person in this world,
one just or pure or altruistic or visionary,
no matter who, or how many, or if only one,
then purity, or justice or mercy or vision,
is something of which matter is capable.
That paradox of the apparent indifference

of matter to such things as Good and Evil,
and, yet, at the same time, the reality
of its complete involvement:
that's why beauty stuns and touches us.
How often you've seen diseased or underfed
people, frail as poplars keening in the wind,
whose matter wishes to die, but spirit keeps them
from snapping nonetheless. It's not only
that we are more than mere matter,
but that matter cannot be so simple as we imagine.
Do you remember that cactus we found
in the desert last year, the one
with a moppet of curly tendrils and quills?

MARÍA
   (Laughs)
Yes.

JUANA
You thought it the most wonderful thing
you'd seen. Why?

MARÍA
It was so outrageous, so unusual.

JUANA
It was a funny predicament for matter
to get into.

MARÍA
Yes.

JUANA
Well, no funnier a predicament
than you, my sweet friend: a heap
of bright fluids, organs, and porridgey things,
all running around within a tight sack
so they don't pour out when you go for a stroll.
   (MARÍA grimaces.)
And a weak stomach!
But when you consider that it's precisely
that porridge and sap from which God makes
all-weather thinkers like Descartes
and Pascal, artists like Botticelli,

that on a pedestal of sticks and stones
sits a mind, and then look at a Botticelli,
how can you not say to yourself:
How amazing that mere matter should lead to this.
And, when you probe matter,
say, a chicken's egg, as we did
yesterday with Dr. Harvey's optick.
How amazing such a thing could result
in a cluck. To explore matter
is to be reminded of beauty,
and beauty matter, which is why study,
though it can be profane,
can also be a means to prayer,
and isn't contrary to modesty and devotion.

MARÍA
To live modestly one needn't think modestly.

JUANA
Exactly.
(She goes to her basket of letters.)
You can fit wide thoughts into a narrow room.
I even think sometimes it may be
the narrow room that widens the thoughts,
like a verse form lacing you up so tightly
you fret harder to turn the right words.
(Opening a letter, she looks surprised.)
This letter is from Giorgio.
But he's due here tomorrow.

MARÍA
Oh, I'm sorry; in my haste,
I didn't recognize his hand.
Ricardo didn't deliver it.

JUANA
Ah, what a sad fate. His father has died
of that plague scalding Europe,
and "plague" they might call it,
no blanket of locusts sucked more green life.
The old are dying caved in and dark,
like milled trees become their own coffins,
children, like ashes, are poofed into oblivion

by the gentlest gust. And the worst part
is it seems to have no moral: good and damned
both are swept away; its black waters
flood full and empty chest alike.

MARÍA
Poor man.

JUANA
Giorgio must return to Turin at once,
to sort out his estate, and provide
for his mother and sisters.
He promises to bring me a new contraption
on his return, and swears that will be soon,
since he fears the unseasonal "climate"
around here of late. Poor Giorgio.
Ah, that will be months, a small forever.

MARÍA
(Sees someone approaching offstage)
Mother Superior!

JUANA
Holy Mother.

MOTHER SUPERIOR
Sister Juana, I've just received
a troubling letter from the Bishop,
which I'm afraid concerns you most
and will greatly alter the lives of us all.

JUANA
What does it say?

MOTHER SUPERIOR
First, he enjoins us to put an end
at once, to all foreign and local visitors
"hanging" as he says "on the rails"
of the convent. "All" and "every" and "at once."
Second, he says our pet dogs must go.

MARÍA
The dogs? Why, there are only six or seven.

MOTHER SUPERIOR
All pet dogs, as they are distractions.

And lastly, well, he has written to you
directly. I'll let you see for yourself.
   (Hands JUANA the letter and a book)
This book seems to be the wood in his blaze.

JUANA
What's this?
What on earth . . . but it doesn't carry my name.

MOTHER SUPERIOR
It doesn't need to.

JUANA
Saints above, it's my conversation
with Father Marceno, after Vespers, months ago,
when he caused me to jot down my thoughts
for his further study.

MOTHER SUPERIOR
Yes, I remember it well.

JUANA
And so I did so, but only because
he commanded me to, and swore
that no other eyes would read it.
Now it looks as if I publicly taunt
the Church Fathers.

MARÍA
The Bishop has always been your ally.

JUANA
But not my armor. And around him
are blades waiting for this opening.
Not least of all the Archbishop.

MOTHER SUPERIOR
A bird of prey
looking for a place to strike.

JUANA
God alone construes him.
   (Reads the letter)
Whew! I don't think Pontius Pilate
gave our Lord such a reprimand.

MOTHER SUPERIOR
Sister!

JUANA
And there's a threat in every line,
like jackals in a closet.
I am to give up all books and counsel
but the Bible, whose devoted study
I have obviously been neglecting.
 (Puts letter down)
What to do. I've much to justify.
I'll straight away send him a reply
so candid, innocent, and heartfelt
that its honesty will be like a ghost
behind a drape, whisper to him from the margins
and win him . . . and weave into the letter
a hundred allusions to theological texts,
each so apt and esoteric that only
a Church scholar impeccable as our Bishop.
will catch them, and thus understand
that I'm not *neglecting* my devotions
but augmenting them.
 (Sits down to write; others leave)

CURTAIN

ACT II, Scene 4

Sister Juana's cell. MARÍA and some other NUNS sneak in while she is away.

MARÍA
She left it over here.
(Rushes to the desk and picks up Juana's reply to BISHOP; begins to read it)

FIRST NUN
Her reply to the Bishop?

MARÍA
Yes, and it's not at all what I'd imagined.
She begins by saying that when she was
born, at midnight, in November of 1648,
she was registered as a "daughter of the Church,"
as her parents were not formally married.

SECOND NUN
No.

FIRST NUN
Go on.

MARÍA
(Paraphrasing)
She grew up in the country,
in the house of her grandfather,
whose library was her fondest passion and toy.
No thing or plea would keep her from it;
so, by three, she had learned to read,
and when, at six or seven, she overheard a guest
mention the university in Mexico City,
she begged her mother to let her go there.
At eight, she wrote a poem to the Eucharist.
Ah, how strange it is . . .
She says that she was so eager to learn
she would punish herself in ways quite strict
for so young a child, for instance,
though she loved cheese, she stopped eating it
because she heard it made one stupid,
and, worst of all, she made a ransom of her hair.

71

FIRST NUN
Goodness, what a will.

SECOND NUN
What an uncommon use of it.

MARÍA
Oh, wait. Here, I have missed a part.

(Reads aloud)
To continue the story of my inclination, which I want you to know all about, I say that I was not yet three years old when my mother sent an older sister of mine to learn to read at one of the schools called Amigas, and partly out of affection, partly out of mischief, I followed her; and when I saw that they were giving her a lesson, I became so inflamed in my desire to learn how to read that I told the teacher, whom I thought I was deceiving, that my mother wanted me to have a lesson. She did not believe it, since it was unbelievable, but in a spirit of good-natured fun she gave me the lesson. I kept going, and she kept teaching me, but it was no longer fun since experience had taught her otherwise; and I learned to read in such a short time that I already knew how before my mother found out, because the teacher had kept it from her in order to surprise her and to receive a reward for her services; and I had kept quiet about it, thinking they would spank me for doing it without their permission. The one who taught me is still living (may God keep her), and she can testify to what I say."

(MARÍA skims the next page.)
Let's see, she says
that at sixteen she was sent to the Viceroy's
palace, to be a lady of the Marquesa de Mancera.
There she learned all the news, fashion,
and intrigues of the court, and surprised everyone
(I am paraphrasing, for she speaks
more modestly than this) with her gentility,
extraordinary learning and wit.
So much so the Marquesa, thinking it a fine circus,
urged her husband to ask in forty professors
from the university to test her.

FIRST NUN
How did she do?

MARÍA

"As a royal galley would against a few canoes."

(NUNS applaud.)

Ah, here she says why she left the court,

when she had there so many suitors.

(Reads aloud)

"I became a nun because although I knew the religious state in life had many things (I mean accessory things, not the formal ones) that were repugnant to my nature, nevertheless, owing to my total disinclination to marriage, it was the most fitting and suitable state I could elect, anxious as I was to assure my salvation. My petty whims were such that I would have preferred to live alone, to have no duty or occupation that might interfere with my freedom for study, to avoid the noise of a community about me which might upset the silence of my books: this was my whim, but whim had to bow down and subject itself to the most important of all: salvation. I vacillated for some time in my determination, but finally some learned persons showed me how my whims were a temptation . . . I thought I was fleeing from myself when I entered the convent; but, wretch that I am, I brought myself with me, and I also brought my worst enemy in this inclination to letters, which (I am not certain) was sent by Heaven either as a gift or a punishment; for, instead of dying down or going out amidst all my religious practices, it blew up like powder . . ."

SECOND NUN

My experience was the same:

to marry and forfeit my freedom,

or come here.

FIRST NUN

And me.

MARÍA

She says she wanted to study Theology,

the queen of the sciences, but to know a queen

one must know the handmaidens first,

so she began to learn Logic, Architecture,

History, Law, Music, and Astronomy.

(Skims a bit)

Here is a bit where she talks

about never having a teacher or fellow students,

the loneliness of being self-taught.

(Reads aloud)

"What might excuse me is the great difficulty I have had, not only in lacking a teacher but in lacking fellow students with whom to discuss and work on the subject matter. My only teacher was a mute book, my only fellow student an inkwell without feeling; and instead of explanations and exercises I had a great many interruptions . . . "

FIRST NUN
How it illuminates the picture
of her and Giorgio.

SECOND NUN
Yes.

MARÍA
(Skimming)
And this is odd. A story of all those
who worked against her studying,
even a prioress who bid her studies be studied
by the Inquisition, and forbade Sister Juana
books for three months, during which time
she was so miserable that, desperate to learn,
she began making her scientific observations.
Other opposition was even nastier.

FIRST NUN
Who? Tell us who.

MARÍA
She refuses to hold up banners against them,
instead she cites the example of Christ,
who was persecuted for being different,
for doing more than most.
(Skims)
. . . The rest of the letter seems to pivot
on complex points of exegesis,
especially of St. Paul's "Let women be quiet
in the church." To press her point,
she gives life to a parade of learned women
of all ages: St. Catherine, St. Gertrude,
Kuan Chin, St. Paula, Hypatia, St. Theresa

of Avila, and others, arguing, or conceding,
perhaps, that women with a wish, a gift, to learn,
should study in private, and not preach in public,
but be allowed to both study and preach.
    (Skimming)
. . . She points out, in passing,
that her two devotional works which were
indeed published, were done so without her
knowledge or consent, or name for that matter.
Otherwise, she has written nothing for publication.
. . . She promises to read more sacred writings,
but
    (María laughs.)
            the letter brims,
like a meniscus on the glass of her mind,
with quotes and allusions to a world
of holy literature, ancient and modern.

SECOND NUN
It's so unlikely a petition.

MARÍA
Yes, the soul-searching is so methodical,
so low-keyed. It stings to read it.

FIRST NUN
Perhaps she meant by it an example,
an aid to others.

MARÍA
Unlike her. And who would see it?
She'd never dream we'd be so devious
as to ransack her wooden nest
like ferrets looking for eggs.
And surely no one will steal it
from the Bishop's cabinet.
No, I think it's for herself
she calls her life into question,
and only incidentally for the Bishop.
She's her own worst examiner,
ready to lop off further inches of hair.

FIRST NUN
Listen, let's make a copy of it
before it's sent, so we can study it
in vacant moments.

MARÍA
Yes, a grand idea.
(She gives them each a few sheets, and all begin to copy.)

CURTAIN

ACT II, Scene 5

A week later, in JUANA's cell. She is posing for a painting by Cabrera.

CABRERA
I confess, Sister Juana, I don't share
your interest in learning German.
To me, it sounds so clotted and rough,
as if a giraffe were choking on an abacus.
They are always clearing their throats
when they speak.
 (Makes guttural sounds)

JUANA
But it's so lapidary and logical,
like adding stones to a cairn,
or building a wall. You don't know
the word for glove, why just plunk down
two word bricks: "hand" "shoe."
Handschuhe. Of course. So logical.
And also, for a woman such as I,
who gabbles like a greyhound,
I like how hard it is to interrupt
a German speaker, virtually impossible:
all the verbs are at the end of the sentence.

CABRERA
Sounds diabolical.

JUANA
Oh, no, what a lovely surprise.
All the while, you hold your breath
and wonder what will this lead to,
and then suddenly there you are
flooded by verbs that make sense of it all.
Imagine the exquisite torment
of German lovers, timid, nervous,
waiting for the verb to tell their fate.

CABRERA
Sister, you have the best way . . .
 (Ricardo runs in, his clothes a mess.)

77

JUANA

(Lets her pose drop)
Ricardo, what's happened to you?
Where's my lord Giorgio?

RICARDO
Oh, Madam!
(Such despair, frustration, and impotence combine in his voice that JUANA sits down.)
We were on board the *St. Teresa,*
bound for the grim business of his father's death,
when, sailing close to the fringe reefs
of the Tortugas, we hit fog and strong currents,
and thus were swept along the coastline.
When we thought for sure we were lost,
what should we see but guide lanterns in the fog,
like coachmen walking on a twilight moor.
Toward those lights we steered, we thought,
out of the shallows when suddenly we hit
broadside upon a reef, and out of the blur
scrambled demons with wild, blood-letting eyes
who had lured us there, to pillage and kill us.
I was knocked overboard when the ship first hit,
and so escaped the butchery I saw . . .

JUANA
What's this strangely embroidered tale?
I asked you, Ricardo, where is my lord?
If, as I take it, he's with you here,
then where's his face? Where is Giorgio?

RICARDO
Oh, Sister, I cannot bear to say it.
He's . . .

JUANA
He's *what*? He's *where*?

RICARDO
Think of the most appalling thing you can.

JUANA
Hurt. Oh, God, he is hurt. But where . . .

RICARDO
Beyond hurt. *Dead,* Sister. I saw it all.

JUANA
Giorgio! You *saw* him killed? You *saw* . . .

RICARDO
Yes, yes, I am certain I did.
　　(Juana moans.)
Later, a fishing ship found me
with some others, but I'm afraid
my beloved lord shed his life there.

JUANA
No, no, it can't be true.

RICARDO
If only it were otherwise,
but he is dead, Madam.
　　(Others withdraw one by one, with RICARDO going last, making a gesture. For a full minute, JUANA pantomimes her upset: clenches her fist, bangs on her chest, gets on her knees and starts thumping the ground with decreasing force. Kneels there. She begins the soliloquy on her knees.)

JUANA
No, not dead, say "lost," but not dead,
say caged with creeping and spitting
jungle horrors that coat the night
like colored vapors on a glass,
but not dead. Dead, so gong-rich
and familiar, the last stroke at midnight
severing every yesterday from today.
The word is the cot of a corpse: dead.
Giorgio, in the bulging cipher
of his grave. Oh, coarse, unsubtle world
to squander such a fortune in the green
bowels of your sea. How shall I walk
from here to there without him,
when the staff of his love led me on,
steadied me. Never again to sit with him
under a night poxed with stars,
never again to find his hand, scuttling

across the blanket like a wayward crab,
never again to gallop through sedgey fields
by his side, a thick vapor of wild scallions
in the air, his laugh realer than the horizon.
"Dead," you said, and not some other word,
some clot of sounds that means reprieve?
Or perhaps I dreamt him and all of it.
　　(Gets up, pauses, then continues)
Once in the courtyard, there, I traced
the shadow of a bird across the grass,
knowing by its shadow it was a bird.
If asked what flew, I would have answered "bird";
but suppose it was a kite, or bit of linen,
suppose it was a leaf, or something else unknown,
a mirage, a stilted wish upon a wing.
There was a man named Giorgio?
A man with whom, and knowledge, I lay
letting the white fever fill me,
whose white fever I could not have said,
so much like brothers were they.
I remember, by the ocean at Veracruz,
tilting my head far back as we loved,
how clouds tumbled across the sky
like bags of light. Once, only sleep
exiled me from him; and, in the morning,
I'd wake to see his hand hovering
over me like a bird of prey
choosing the best place to land.
　　(Pauses)
How shall I inquire, when he was so curious?
How be merciful, when he was so kind?
How create, when he was so full of art?
How eat and drink without the tonic
of his charm? No, the busier I am
the more I will think of him.
Look there, that light dancing on the floor
like a trembling beast. Even the light
has life, and Giorgio has none.
Giorgio dead, and in a carnal circus,
prey to all the mauve hucksters of the deep
who are silently conning him

80

out of his cells, under a wide green wink.
The filthiest snout in a burrow has life,
black scabs rolling bits of dung have life,
a clamshell tied together by a yawn,
mosquitos stilting disease across a pond,
mean men bellying from their dens to strike,
my God, even witless plants
droning green anthems in the sun
have life! Count and critter have life!
And Giorgio is dead. Say the world has stopped,
time floats like a scum on dead water,
time swirls like a collop of sand.
My world that seemed so rich before him,
once I knew him, was not enough.
It changed from a moss that lived
only on air to an orient of petals.
On the long peninsula of my life,
in whose swamps and meadows flocked tribes
of gorgeous, low-nesting birds,
suddenly love built an aviary—
gone now, flooded back to the sea.
Motion is all, and he will be inert.
He will be a lull where a life was.
He will be a neverthriving of hopes.
He will be less than an inkling.
His mind that could contemplate itself, even,
won't contemplate the shy hooves
of a goat. What is life,
that it could include this misery,
as well as those radiant flowers outside?
Giorgio is gone, beyond wish,
beyond dredging, and I am alone again
with my solitary mania, but worse,
for knowing it could be otherwise.
Death, that drank the sun from his sky,
you may as well come feast on mine:
scrape off the colored bark of daylight,
and milk the lilies of the night,
for, like Giorgio, I'm lost at sea,
watching, helpless, as the world empties.
    (Others return, as she sways; RICARDO catches her.)

CABRERA
When one bookend is pulled away,
how could the other keep its footing?
(Commotion offstage. MOTHER SUPERIOR rushes in.)

MOTHER SUPERIOR
Sister, Sister, you must come at once!
His Eminence has sent three Holy Fathers.
They say they come to examine us
on our faith . . . What's this?
(Speaking simultaneously)

RICARDO
She has . . .

CABRERA
Perhaps they . . .

JUANA
I'll go with the other Sisters.
They will need me. Indeed, what does it matter now.
Ricardo, leave by the window, hurry,
and find my brother at Veracruz,
who'll give you work.

RICARDO
Madam, if only I . . .

JUANA
You are not the news you bring.
Go quickly, before they come, loyal friend.
(RICARDO leaves by the window. MOTHER SUPERIOR leaves.)
Giorgio, my other rib, is dead,
and now this. I'll fight them as best I can.
They won't have me! . . . Or perhaps they will.
Ah, Cabrera, dear friend, I feel like Pandora
at the end of the box, with a world
full of misery and evil set loose.
All that remains for me now is hope.

CABRERA
(To himself)
And that can be the worst of all.

CURTAIN

ACT III, Scene 1

ARCHBISHOP sits in a chair at the corner of the stage, the rest of which is in blackness. His face looks ghoulish and contorted, like a painting by Francis Bacon. He holds a medieval book.

ARCHBISHOP
I am no Ramses flogging the nuns of Zion
to heap blocks of stone in a wilderness
of faith. I am no rod of the Lord,
from whose cap pour plagues of toad and locust,
but a mild, much-maligned, faithful servant
of the Lord, who must answer for many souls
in this province. She wishes to learn?
Let her learn! I don't object to her learning.
"The hearing ear and the seeing eye,
the Lord hath made both of them," says Matthew.
If only she would do it discreetly
in the convent's shade, away from the hot
wicked humors of the world,
if only she would do it in moderation:
sip some learning to be cordial perhaps,
but not grow drunk, wild, and unruly from it.
A woman should take the pill of knowledge
in half doses, lest it strain her soft nature,
lest it roughen her mild ways
with a too-manly appetite, lest it bud
in her like the gland of a civet
and attract the lower senses that slobber
and quicken, repelling the pure.
   I have met this odd bird at prayer
and on the street, and her knowledge
is a growth, a club foot she drags; it stumbles
from under her robes as she walks.
Nor should a mind so amply equipped
for broad faith and the wider sea of salvation
drag to port in every barrio of the world
to career with roustabouts, fools,
and nay-sayers, in the petty hovels
and refuse heaps of a common life.
In a lesser mind, it would be a lesser folly.
They are all trouble, these raucous birds,

who come direct from court and high families,
direct from the spoils and petting
of duped fathers to dance into their vows,
believing they can wheedle salvation from God
as if it were an extra sweet or new ribbon.

Like horseleeches, these daughters
cry only "Give, Give." But the path to salvation
is overgrown, and the jungles snarled high.
They must learn to chop through evil
without wincing, slash at temptation,
scrape away the private poisons
and cleanse the wound with fire,
these women who are born with wounds
in which their own blood rains
like a holocaust every month,
thanks to the disobedience of Eve.
They return to her wickedness,
these unholy sisters wrapped all in black,
like rats lurking in their own shadows.
How they sink their teeth
into the apple of the church,
and wish to drive the manly body of the law
to spill itself on the ground for them.
They taint its pure spirit with their fetid blood,
with their filthy, pouring volcanos inside.
That life could hatch in such a mire—
it's disgusting! Like goslings
born out of a swollen, smelly marsh.

You can't put pure wine into a corrupt bottle,
and expect it to stay sweet. No, no.
This sister, she needs to be purified,
purified by a worm, a worm of terror
with a long, spiny maw below her gut
working its icy mischief as she sleeps;
she needs to have the cross burned on her tongue
so each word will be cleansed
by the agony of our Lord; she needs
to be stuffed with lilies dipped in holy oil,
and then the cave of her disgrace sewn shut.
I will make her pure as a benediction,
so she's fit again for men's eyes,

snowy, clean, bloodless, and unstained,
a single white candle burning its wax
on the altar. I will crush the pearl in her hips,
and turn her poppy-red gush
into a single beating faith.
I will blank out the farting trumpet
of her studies, and distill her bubbly spirit
to still wine. I will take an axe
and strike at the root of her,
where false prophets build a tabernacle
and virtue is razed.
Will she squirm? Then I will fasten her
like a nail to a sure place,
so she will not escape, or her flesh will stay.
I will rash her unholy, sin-charred limbs
with a shirt of my own hair
until she begs me to flog her,
questing for pain like a perfect rose.
I will make her soul jump from her body
like a shadow from the sparkling glare
of sunlit water. I will heat her will
like iron in a forge, bend her into a shape
fit for salvation, and quench her slowly,
in stages, the last as she quivers,
deep into the sacred blue vat of Heaven.

   (Crosses the stage)
Father Odon, the reformer at the Abbey
of Cluny, even in 1100, he knew.

   (Reads aloud from a book)
"Indeed, if men were endowed, like the lynxes
of Boetia, with the power of visual penetration
and could see what there is beneath the skin,
the mere sight of women would nauseate them:
that feminine grace is only saburra, blood,
humor, bile. Consider what is hidden in
the nostrils, in the throat, in the belly:
filth everywhere . . . How can we desire to hold
in our arms the bag of excrement itself?''

   (Closes the book and continues off stage, mumbling)
He knew, he knew.

(Lights come up. Several NUNS, stricken by the plague, loiter around the corners of the stage but are not in the action of the stage. A stark chamber. No books or apparatuses. JUANA sits, staring into the middle distance, a rosary in her hand. On the table lies a hair shirt and a penitent's whip. MARÍA and another young NUN stand off to one side, speaking.)

MARÍA
She has been like this now for nearly a year.
Her cell is still intact, but locked
by Bishop's order, which also forbids her
any book, save a Bible, nor apparatuses
save hair shirts and other penitential things.
He moved her here, to this narrow room,
which, shaped like a line, would greater make
his point.

NUN
She doesn't look well.

MARÍA
Nor is. Without her books, she soon grew ill.
They were her food, and kept her spirits sleek.
A small book, no larger than a leaf,
could power her for endless days and nights.
The other food, what little she takes, does little.

NUN
Perhaps it was poor Giorgio's death?

MARÍA
I'm like an observer in the wake
of two tempests, unable to say which
did the worse damage. Both storms hit at once,
and, when they'd passed, all that remained
was fine wreckage: planks and seaweed,
the husk of a hull, what you see before you.

NUN
Ricardo?

MARÍA
He went to work for her brother,
building ships at Veracruz.

86

Once half of Europe sailed through this harbor,
and now only those with dying relations come.
Some say the plague is God's punishment of her,
to seize by death all her pupils.

NUN
All are gone?

MARÍA
Only I and three others remain,
two of them stricken. When she moves,
it's to nurse them lovingly, as she has
all the others dying these last months.

NUN
She says nothing?

MARÍA
Only her prayers and devotions.
Quizzed about matters of the mind,
art or science, she renounces them
venemously, as if the Bishop barked.
They pretend to have driven the demon
from her, but the monster that now consumes her
is worse, leeching out her zest and ideas,
and leaving only the pale carcass you see.
    (JUANA faints. MARÍA and NUN run to her.)
Sister! Oh! Look, the disease
building its tents on her barren face.
Quickly, run for the doctor and Mother Superior.
    (The other NUN runs out.)

JUANA
Who's left?

MARÍA
Only a visitor, Sister.

JUANA
Ah, yes, only a visitor. Just so.
It drops by one morning in a wail of sunlight,
then steals away in darkness,
leaving behind all its baggage and woe.
Only a visitor, going.

MARÍA

Sister, don't speak, save your strength
to fight the disease.

MARÍA

No, not at ease, but as lonely
as God alone must feel. Giorgio gone,
my books, my arts, my pupils, my friends.
To lose a life is small compared to that.
To lose a life *is* all of that,
and little more, if precious little,
offal even disease won't touch:
yards of idleness, the fish-hooks
that make a whim, the body's palate
when flesh unbends, maddening beauty
and saner bouts of terror like repeat blows
of the same fist. "Hath the rain a father?
Who has begotten the drops of dew?"

MARÍA

(Looking anxiously off stage)
Where are they?

JUANA

"There arises a little cloud
out of the sea, like a man's hand."
Lord, lead me to the rock that is higher
than I am. My Lord, if now I find favor
in thy sight, pass not away from thy servant.

MARÍA

Sister, be strong, and calm. Oh, Sweet Jesus.
I'll be gone only a moment.
(Runs off stage)

JUANA

Sweet Jesus, a moment.
The plague that scumbles me, which is it now?
The older plague we take from birth?
The black that was before the stars were?
The plague of my willfulness
that bid me look when faith said listen,
that bid me ask when faith said believe,

88

that bid me love when faith said be pure,
that bid me marvel when faith said be still?
The bug that frightened them, I sought.
It lived in me, I gave it work;
and now it eats the larder bare.
"The heart is deceitful above all things,
and desperately wicked, who can know it?"
   (MARÍA returns with MOTHER SUPERIOR, a DOCTOR, and the VISITING NUN.)
Who's there?

MARÍA
Only María, Mother, and your friends.

JUANA
No, no, dead, I'd forgotten. And wrong.
Sweet loaves of denial. My strength,
it's made perfect in this weakness.
Long after the skin-worms unfurl my body,
in every sinew I'll know God well.
I hear good news from a far country.

MARÍA
Sweet Sister.

JUANA
Who's there, shaking the bridle of my cells?
   (MOTHER SUPERIOR takes up her rosary and prays quietly.)
Ah, Father, it's you, backing me
into my grave so there's no more balking.
Lead on, you've been a stranger so long.
Who's there? What? Sea lilies. Falling.
I am. Sweet dreams of reason. No more.
Swirling black. Oh! Sunlit meadow, sweet grass.

MARÍA
   (Crying)
Sister, teacher, friend.
   (PRIEST arrives to give last rites.)

CURTAIN

ACT III, Scene 2

In Juana's original cell. Cobwebs. Few books and experiments. A painting half-finished. She lies in her bed, around which stand MARÍA, the VISITING NUN, the MOTHER SUPERIOR, the BISHOP, and a clergyman. The lights are dim. The CLERGY-MAN, swinging a censer as he recites Latin liturgy for a short spell. The BISHOP makes a cross in the air above JUANA. Suddenly GIORGIO enters with RICARDO, and the stage lights come up a little. MARÍA runs to them.

MARÍA
My Lord, what a miracle! We thought you dead.

GIORGIO
I well may be. There are moments
when my knees go numb, my throat seems full
of congealed lead, and I have nothing to say,
nothing to do, I want to hear from no one,
be no one. I catch myself going through the motions
like a marionette wishing his strings would break.

MARÍA
Nonetheless, and by Heaven's grace,
you're alive. I don't think I could have endured
losing you both.
   (Trembles)

GIORGIO
You're shaking, María.

MARÍA
It's seeing the ghost of you.
We thought you dead. What happened?

GIORGIO
Happened. What a strange relief it is
to tell how one *almost* died.
It makes you feel you did die once,
and while Death was out wooing a new colt,
or a daughter, you crept back into life.
And I did, too, floating on wreckage
for five days, not daring to drink
what surrounded me, in my delirium dreaming

90

I was here in this cell, and in saner fits
certain I would never see it again;
until by chance the current carried me south
to a small island of the Misteriosa chain,
where the sea boils with enormous turtles.
There the natives revived me, and for months
I had to wait until at last a turtling ship
passed by, and agreed to carry me to Veracruz.
When we docked, high up a mast, repairing
a crow's nest, was none other than Ricardo,
whom I'd guessed dead, as he had me;
though to hear his news of Juana
I drowned a hundred times on that dock.
I would sooner have died ragged in a jaw
on the sea, while beaked fish plucked
my entrails apart, than survive to learn this.

BISHOP
My Lord of Turin, we thought you dead.

GIORGIO
And if the coils of thought had venom,
I'd be so.
   (Sees JUANA)
How the disease has changed her.
Even to see her face blackened like that—
still she's beautiful: an Ethiopian queen.
The world loses its keenest soul.

BISHOP
And Heaven gains a purified one.
It may interest you to know that,
in her last days, her expiation was complete,
strict, abstinent, and fitting.
Devotion was her rule and measure.
She renounced all, even you finally,
taking heart in God's glory and her salvation.

GIORGIO
Gentle soul, what must they
have put you through?
   (Looks around her study)

What will become of all her books, arts,
and experiments?

BISHOP
As the Church was her support,
her goods pass to it.

GIORGIO
And all the messengers with news,
the savants, supplicants, and callers
who swarm daily for the honey of her thought,
who will tell the hive of them she's dead?

BISHOP
None come. They were released
from that fealty long ago.

GIORGIO
Fealty, how dare you speak of fealty,
having taxed her more than her plot
on this earth.

BISHOP
She had false prophets; she lost her way.
Mortal life is like a fog:
before you enter it, the air is crisp,
pure, and wholesome, then you're in the foul of it,
with no sense where you are, or what life
truly looks like, until you leave,
when the air shines clear again.
"Lay not up for yourself treasures upon the earth, where moth
and rust corrupt, and thieves break through to steal.
Lay up for yourself treasures in Heaven,"
saieth Matthew.

*(Voices speak from across the centuries. Though they come
from off-stage, the BISHOP thinks they are GIORGIO speaking.)*

FIRST VOICE
There was something supernatural,
almost miraculous, about her appearing
during such an age.

SECOND VOICE
She was a woman, with a woman's walk

and a woman's ways.

THIRD VOICE
She had knowledge of everything,
she wrote about everything,
and it was on everything she left her mark.

BISHOP
You speak as though time were funnelling
through your voice.

GIORGIO
For a slim mind, a life is a slim thing,
I suppose, held like a scream
between the dirt and the sky, exiled
to the present as if to one shore
rocking in an archipelago of dreams.
She knew a wider life, if not a longer one.
Her friends leapt from their pages
to be with her. She spoke with them.
Others will speak with her.

BISHOP
They'll have to do so in Heaven.

GIORGIO
In the Heaven of their hope,
from the fog of their despair.
Such a being. She could stain the willows
with a glance. She knew so well,
in her cells, on her pulse, how it felt
to have once been alive on this planet.
In her verses, you can hear
the warm summer winds, *hush,*
rustling *hush* through the trees,
and brooks sizzling as if they were
frying fish. She was so human.

BISHOP
Human! You drop the word into the slops of your emotion as if it
were a compliment.
Human is corrupt. Human is deluded.
Human is full of sin, folly, and disgust.

She overreached; she was willful and obstinate.
Her misfortune was to be shot through
with avarice. "The disciple is not above
his master, nor the servant above his lord."
"The doors shall be shut in the streets,
when the sound of the grinding is low,
and he shall rise up at the voice of the bird,
and all the daughters of music shall be brought low."

GIORGIO
Her misfortune . . . I suppose it was
to be alive at all in this age,
with the continent astir, and these colonies
astir, and scientists in every country
banging the world's drum, as if on a snipe hunt,
and the Church at odds to keep order and quiet.
The world heaving a new shape into the light,
and mad fibers dragging it down again.
It was the windswept edge of the untried
that excited her; but life along the edge
pays dearly.

BISHOP
Bah! There's no use knocking on your door,
when she's so clearly witched it shut.
But mind you watch your almighty soul:
to defend her disobedience is to share in it.
Keep on as you are, and you'll find
the weeds around you rising up like daggers,
despite your dispensation at court.

GIORGIO
I am well warned, and, as you see,
so scalded by grief that my words
come out sounding hotter than they're meant.
Give it no mind, but do grant me
a moment alone with her.
    (BISHOP considers.)
To pay my last respects.
What futher harm could it do?
    (BISHOP and others leave.)
Ricardo, stay.

(He does.)

How could I have come too late to save her?
The thought will impale me till I drop,
which will be soon, if the mercy that missed her
finds me. But perhaps I'm still in time
to save something of her.

(Goes to her desk, searches the drawers)
In this desk,
she used to store her writings.

(Takes out a sheet of paper and reads aloud)

"To a Linnet
Crimson cithern, as the daylight broke,
trilled a song for his beloved spouse,
fed her the sweet amber of the rose,
splashed and coral-stained her golden beak.

Sweetest linnet, mournful little wing:
scarcely had he seen the enchanted dawn
than, at the first full throttle of a tune,
he discovered death, and lost his song.

There is in life no moment fixed for death;
his very voice beckoned the marksman on,
who, when he struck, was full sure of aim.
O fortune sought for, yet we fear your wrath!

Who could foretell the song that hailed the sun
would be the accomplice of the singer's doom?"

(GIORGIO puts down the poem.)
Oh, "mournful little wing," that you could write
your own epitaph at such a time.

(Picks up a sack and fills it with her papers)
Ricardo, take this bundle
and head back to the coast, there board
a ship for Italy. I will meet you in Genoa
at Dr. Redi's. Wait for me there.

RICARDO
I will.

GIORGIO
Until you reach the coast,

travel only by night; you carry with you
a lava brighter than the sun,
and her enemies would douse you both
if they knew it.

RICARDO
On my life, they won't. You'll find me in Genoa,
safely waiting with her thoughts.

GIORGIO
Her thoughts will have travelled with me,
as well. Hurry, then, good friend.
   (RICARDO leaves by the window.)
My lovely linnet, what I'd give
to see your black wings fluttering now.
Until we meet again elsewhere,
or elsewhen. If it's in Heaven,
then, as you said, it will have to go far
to outgallop this Eden; if it's less
than Heaven, for me it will be Heaven—
like an alchemist's fluid, you'll pour
into that world and transmute its baseness
to gold just by being there.
But if it's neither? Oh, dreadful thought.
Can it be that we pass out of nothing
into nothing, and between them runs
all the pant and lather of life,
fetching the sticks of love, worry, sickness,
for no master? No, no, I dare not think it.
If life shatters all, nothing remains
but filings of a human sort
to bake, loaf-quiet, in a cold oven,
where no bones rise, and the senses leaven.
Broken dinghies, days without Juana—
how can I float a heavy cargo on ether?
Surely death will not rob us till we're chaste
and hollow. If life shatters all,
what hope has the swallow?
What hope have I, if her heart squalls
no longer, her gift's recalled,
even our rapid love has stalled,
and, blind as a hammer, life shatters all?

I must not, I will not believe it.
It would be unbearable, to have no chance
together in no ampler time.
If only . . . if only . . . an armada of onlies,
each nothing more than a small perhaps,
and yet together they wage a battle
with my sanity. If only you had loved me more,
or I had loved you less.
  (Church bells begin.)
Farewell, I must go to Genoa.
This world has such a draft in it now.
  (He leaves as RICARDO did. Church bells finish striking as the lights dim.)

CURTAIN

Lumen Books

Dialogue in the Void: Beckett and Giacometti
Matti Megged
ISBN: 0-9930829-01-8, $7.95

Culture and Politics in Nicaragua:
Testimonies of Poets and Writers
Steven White

Under a Mantle of Stars
A Play in Two Acts
Manuel Puig
Translated by Ronald Christ
ISBN: 0-930829-00-X, $6.95

Space in Motion
Juan Goytisolo
Translated by Helen Lane
ISBN: 0-930829-03-4, $8.95

Sor Juana's Dream
Luis Harss
ISBN: 0-930829-07-7, $9.95

For an Architecture of Reality
Michael Benedikt
ISBN: 0-930829-05-0, $9.95

Borges in/and/on Film
Edgardo Cozarinsky
Translated by
Gloria Waldman & Ronald Christ
ISBN: 0-930829-08-5, $10.95

Angst Cartography
Moji Baratloo & Clif Balch
ISBN: 0-930829-10-7, $8.95

The remarkable Juana Inés de la Cruz, a woman tragically and triumphantly ahead of her time, comes to life again in Diane Ackerman's eloquent, witty, and poignant drama, **Reverse Thunder.**

Working now in fact, now in imagination, Ms. Ackerman recreates both an admirable and credible Juana and, at the same time, her exciting intellectual milieu: the world of the late seventeenth century.

And she does it in grand style, the truly grand style of Elizabethan rhetoric, the perfect language for this dramatic poem of intellectual excitement, physical passion, and priestly machination.

Only Diane Ackerman, a sister spirit of this seventeenth-century sister, could have woven so rich a fabric into this dramatic poem. A brilliant poet, a writer of natural history, an aviator, an explorer of the arcane, and a polymath in her own right, she is the creative historian and biographer for whom this subject has been waiting all these years.

Philip Appleman
*Distinguished Professor of English,
Indiana University*

Diane Ackerman has published three collections of poetry, *Lady Faustus, Wife of Light, The Planets: A Cosmic Pastoral,* and two works of nonfiction, *On Extended Wings* and *Twilight of the Tenderfoot.* Her essays in natural history and other topics appear in periodicals such as *The New Yorker* and *The New York Times.*

ISBN 0-930829-09-3